# EXPERT PROFILES

## VOLUME 2

Conversations with Influencers & Innovators

# EXPERT PROFILES
## VOLUME 2
### Conversations with Influencers & Innovators


Featuring:


Matt Mitchell

Nayeli Gómez

Julie A. Stein

Lorri Silvera

Batista Gremaud

Patty L. Cummings

Darren Coleman

Copyright © 2018 Authority Media Publishing

Published by Authority Media Publishing Houston, TX

The Publisher has strived to be as accurate and complete as possible in the creation of this book.

This book is not intended for use as a source of legal, business, accounting or financial advice. All readers are advised to seek services of competent professionals in legal, business, accounting, medical, and financial fields.

In practical advice books, like anything else in life, there are no guarantees of income made. Readers are cautioned to rely on their own judgment about their individual circumstances and to act accordingly.

While all attempts have been made to verify information provided in this publication, the Publisher assumes no responsibility for errors, omissions, or contrary interpretation of the subject matter herein. Any perceived slights of specific persons, peoples, or organizations are unintentional.

Expert Profiles Volume 2 – 1st ed.
ISBN: 978-1-946694-12-6

Royalties from the Retail Sales of "Expert Profiles" are
donated to Global Autism Project

**AUTISM KNOWS NO BORDERS;**
FORTUNATELY NEITHER DO WE.®

Global Autism Project 501(c)3, is a nonprofit organization which provides training to local individuals in evidence-based practices for individuals with autism.

Global Autism Project believes that every child has the ability to learn and their potential should not be limited by geographical bounds.

The Global Autism Project seeks to eliminate the disparity in service provision seen around the world by providing high-quality training to individuals providing services in their local community. This training is made sustainable through regular training trips and contiguous remote training.

You can learn more about Global Autism Project by visiting GlobalAutismProject.org.

# Table of Contents

# Creating Unforgettable Memories for Your Dream Wedding

Matt Mitchell is the founder of Mitchell Event Planning based in Atlanta, GA. He is a Certified Wedding Planner™ through the Association of Bridal Consultants, one of the largest and oldest groups of wedding professionals in the United States. Mitchell Event Planning specializes in wedding planning and coordination, in turn, helping couples navigate the complex planning process and ensuring flawless day of execution.

## Conversation with Matt Mitchell

*Tell us a little bit about Mitchell Event Planning and how you are helping couples turn their dream wedding into a reality.*

**Matt Mitchell**: Mitchell Event Planning specializes in wedding planning and coordination. We partner with newly-engaged couples to make sure that their most important day goes smoothly.

We offer services from full planning, which starts at day one, all the way to the coordination, which is the day-of, to make sure the execution of their wedding is flawless.

Typically, I like to see clients at least a year in advance. There are aspects that need to be thought of in that timeframe. An example would be availability at venues for the clients' specific wedding date. Another thing to consider is the wedding dress. Many brides don't realize that dresses are not typically bought off the rack; they are generally custom-made. The customization can take up to six months depending on where it is made and around what holiday(s) it is ordered. The earlier the couple starts planning their wedding, the better, and I like to get involved as quickly as possible. I have had couples come to me six months out from their wedding day, and all they have is a venue, with nearly 70% of their budget spent. This is not an ideal situation; however, I can still help! When we get involved early, it will alleviate issues like that and ensure the budget is correctly allocated.

When people think about weddings, their mind usually goes to more of a traditional ceremony. Our current environment is quite different, as you see couples taking their own spin on these traditions. I do like to educate my clients and provide meaning behind the tradition, but do not expect them to incorporate all within their wedding day. I like to partner with my clients and really get to know them on a personal level, and capture their unique characteristics to customize a wedding that speaks of them. I like to build in both individual characteristics and their characteristics as a couple. It is the first time that they are introducing themselves, officially, as a couple to the world. The guests at their wedding are the first people to get to see them together in that light, thus, I feel having a wedding that is customized to them is very important.

*What are the most common problems you see couples running into during their wedding planning process?*

**Matt Mitchell**: A major problem that people often overlook is how much a wedding is going to actually cost, or if they know, they don't take the appropriate steps to make sure that they stay on budget. This is another area in which I can really add value. I have a finance background, so I can easily create a budget and manage it to ensure it does not get out of hand. There were some stats recently released for the Atlanta area: people expected their budget to be around $13,000, but ended up spending $24,000, which is 185% over the proposed budget! Unfortunately, this is common, so budgeting is one thing that I focus on when working with my clients.

I have partnerships with all types of venues and vendors throughout the Atlanta area. I can tap into those partnerships and find a fit for my clients that will be within their budget.

*What are some other costs that should be considered when planning a wedding?*

**Matt Mitchell**: Couples will have to factor in all of their other vendor fees, not just the venue. Typical vendors include: Planner/Designer, Photographer/Videographer, Baker, Caterer, DJ/Band, Instrumentalist/Vocalist, Stationary, Lighting, Decor/Rentals, Florist, Hair/Make-up Artist, etc.

Some other considerations would be attire, for both the bride and groom. Most couples also provide gifts to their wedding party and favors to their wedding guests.

I find that many couples do not take into consideration everything that needs to be budgeted for. Often, couples do not rely on a planner until later in their planning process when they feel overwhelmed or stuck. There is a lot that goes into planning that many people do not think about. I find I can add a lot of value by meeting vendors with my couples, reviewing contracts, and negotiating, if needed. This can provide big savings to my couples and ensure they are not surprised with any last-minute expenses.

*The wedding day can be extremely stressful, especially for the bride. How does having a wedding planner help to keep everything calm or reduce that stress as much as possible?*

**Matt Mitchell**: Even though many brides are very organized and have a true vision of what they want, the wedding day is one of the most stressful days of their lives. They have been planning for so long to make sure that everything is right, but do not have time to oversee the day. They are busy with hair/make-up, getting in their dress, taking pictures, etc. If they hire a Planner or even a Day-Of Coordinator, all that stress can be taken away, and they can focus on just being a bride.

One of the most important things that I do is the Day-Of Coordination. I am there the entire wedding day for the bride, groom, family, friends, vendors, etc. I arrive in the morning to supervise load in with the vendors, ensure the decorations are setup correctly, and keep everyone on schedule. I create a timeline for the day and serve as the contact for all the vendors - any questions/concerns come to me and not to the bride. I find that being the "go to" person really alleviates the stress on not only the bride, but the groom and their families.

Not only do the vendors get a timeline, but so does the bridal party, the groomsmen, and the family. It is a very orchestrated operation and important to keep on track. Often, when you are at a venue, simply going over an hour can incur a fee. That is also the case with many vendors, if you keep anyone longer than the contracted time, then you will be charged extra. That is the type of scenario I keep from happening. I make sure everything is on track and runs smoothly.

*What are some of the biggest myths out there around planning a wedding?*

**Matt Mitchell**: A lot of people feel that they can plan everything themselves, and admittedly there are couples that successfully do this. As in most things, people can "figure it out." However, the end result tends to not be the best quality or even the easiest process for those involved. It is important to hire a skilled professional. I am a Certified Wedding Planner™ through the Association of Bridal Consultants and receive continuing education every year. I attend workshops, seminars, and networking events - all to ensure I'm keeping up with wedding trends, couple preferences, etc. This also allows me to connect with vendors of all types throughout the Atlanta area and the Southeast. It is important to build relationships with people within the wedding industry. I have the opportunity to work with them and ensure that my clients get a skilled professional that will provide a great end product and client experience. These relationships also ensure my clients are getting the best pricing available.

*When couples are flipping through the magazines, thinking about what their wedding will be like, do they ever worry that a wedding planner might not be able to capture their vision of the big day?*

**Matt Mitchell**: This is something that has been vocalized in the past. The couples I have experienced this with thought they could do it on their own. They were apprehensive to bring in a wedding planner because they felt their vision would not be captured, or that it would be easier for them to create it.

This is the reason I like to take a partnership approach to planning and design. I want to make sure what they have envisioned comes to life. I take the time to meet with the couples many times to get to know them–not even specifically to talk about the wedding, but to really get to know them. I like to know where they came from, what they are looking to do, and what they have envisioned for themselves after marriage. The creative part is building those details into their wedding design.

*What are some of the misconceptions about hiring an event planner or a wedding planner to take care of that big day?*

**Matt Mitchell**: I think some people feel planners are too costly and that they can save money by doing everything on their own. When it comes to pricing - there are some planners that will take a percentage of the budget. I do not structure my pricing like that. I build custom quotes for each couple based on the level of service they truly need/want. I like to be flexible and transparent, so if we agree on one thing and it looks like maybe they can't afford it or they need even more than previously thought - I will restructure our agreement to be in line with the couple's needs. As previously mentioned, I like to get to know the couple, what they have done so far, and what they truly need from me. This ensures they get the most bang for their buck and that they're getting the amount of service that they need, but also that they can afford.

*It sounds like using a wedding planner can actually be financially beneficial to a couple since they already have working relationships and can help with vendor contract negotiations.*

**Matt Mitchell**: Absolutely! There are a lot of things that go into the contracts and when you don't have the knowledge, things can get overlooked. There is also an opportunity to talk to the vendor(s) and negotiate for a discount or other non-monetary perks. For example, at a venue, I can look to negotiate a free night stay and/or get the couple's guests a better rate at the hotel, etc. Partnerships are crucial in business and I will say that it is a tight-knit community when it comes to wedding professionals in the Atlanta area. Most planners have a list of preferred vendors in which they can easily present to our couples. Ultimately, the decision is up to the couple which vendor(s) they want to hire, but I can provide them with different options and different price points based on their budget.

*What are some of the fears you see couples face when planning their wedding or making the decision to use a wedding planner?*

**Matt Mitchell**: One fear is that wedding planners are too expensive. That may be the case in some instances, but couples must find a planner that works for them. Planners have different philosophies and different fee structures. It is very important for couples to interview their wedding planner to make sure that it is a good fit, not only for them, but for the planner. We are in the digital age, so we do a lot on our phones and through email. I always have a face-to-face meeting with my couples before any kind of contract is presented. I want to make sure that the chemistry is there and that I can provide them what they are looking for. I believe that a connection on a personal level is important when entering into a business relationship. There are plenty of options out there. If one planner is a little over their price point, or maybe they are not connecting well with them - continue interviewing, there are options out there to fit any couple's needs.

Another fear couples have voiced is specifically on the wedding day. One example is the chance of rain for an outdoor wedding. This is nothing to fear, but something you must take into consideration throughout the planning process. It is crucial to have a backup plan in place. There is always the fear that everything won't be perfect, but that fear can be calmed when you are prepared and organized.

*What's the most common mistake or pitfall that can be avoided when trying to plan a wedding?*

**Matt Mitchell**: Generally, it comes down to time. A year sounds like a long time, but when you have so much to do, that year flies by. Getting started early can make the planning process go by much smoother. Something I do for my couples is sending them a monthly to-do list. It is not necessarily to-dos for them, but it provides transparency around what we need to accomplish for that month. It can provide them a comforting feeling as they check off important milestones in the planning process. Giving yourself enough planning time will make the process less stressful and can help make the process even more fun.

*Things don't always go as planned. Is there a wedding that stands out as an example of how you have dealt with unexpected obstacles and still delivered a memorable day for your newlyweds?*

**Matt Mitchell**: Recently a couple had a destination wedding in Panama City Beach, Florida. This wedding was in October, which you might recall is hurricane season. On the wedding day, Hurricane Nate was making landfall just to the West of Panama City. The bride had envisioned a beach wedding, but the weather was threatening to intervene into that plan. I went out to the beach one hour before the wedding to ensure everything was set up. When I came back, 30 minutes later, all of the set up was underwater! The tide had risen, the waves were crashing in, and there was barely any beach left.

We had to make a last-minute decision on whether we were going to have a beach wedding or use the backup venue. The bride was dead set on getting married on the beach. Although it wasn't as planned, we made it happen! They didn't get married under the arbor and there were no chairs for people to sit on, but the guests were able to stand along the boardwalk and watch the ceremony. The couple and the wedding party were able to get on what was left of the beach to say their vows and have their first kiss. We made it back to the house where the reception took place. In the backyard, we had a big tent that had all the tables and chairs under it. Despite the threat of Hurricane force winds and tropical rain, it turned out to be a beautiful evening.

Maybe it wasn't the dream wedding on the beach that she had envisioned, but she did achieve her beach wedding and she still talks about it today.

*What inspired you to become a wedding planner?*

**Matt Mitchell**: I started out as a wedding singer where I would perform in either the reception or the ceremony. It was here that I fell in love with weddings. It is a day that you get to spend with two people that are about to commit their lives to each other. They have put so much time and energy into the day, and it is a labor of love to make a wedding happen. Those instances really spoke to me and it was something that I became very interested in. I had experience in corporate event planning, so I had the background when it comes to making sure a day is executed correctly. However, it was the weddings that really spoke to me.

There is a lot more passion in wedding planning than in corporate event planning, because it means so much more to the client. It's a personal time and they not only hire you, but they invite you into their most important day. It is something that I cherish, and I take it very seriously. I want to make sure that I'm capturing exactly what they have envisioned. I believe that love is love and envision a world that is all inclusive. I want to be a leader in the Industry, and provide services for all clients–regardless of gender, sexual orientation, race, religion, etc. It was with those beliefs and a desire to provide the best client experience that I decided to make it official–and Mitchell Event Planning was born.

*It's got to be rewarding for you to be a part of such an important day in so many people's lives. What should people look for as they consider and evaluate a wedding planner to play such a role in their big day?*

**Matt Mitchell**: It is so rewarding and I am thankful I get to do this as a job. When considering a wedding planner, it is very important to meet and personally interview them. There are great websites out there for you to compare vendors, so I would suggest people begin there: look at their work, look on Instagram and Facebook, go to their website, read reviews, and look at their portfolio to see the caliber of work that they can provide. This will get you to a short list, and at that point you can start making your inquiries. You have found the people that you are interested in, now you can start narrowing down the people that are in your price point. Once you have narrowed it down to your top three, start interviewing them.

I would encourage you to meet with them face-to-face, not just over the phone or through emails. Sit down with them, make sure your personalities match and that you feel you can trust them with your day. It is a very important partnership, so it's very important that you get it right.

# About Matt Mitchell

Matt Mitchell, is no stranger to the wedding/event planning business. Matt is a native Alabamian and graduate of The University of Alabama with a Bachelor's of Science in Commerce and Business Administration. He is a Certified Wedding Planner™ and proud member of the largest group of wedding professionals, The Association of Bridal Consultants. Matt created Mitchell Event Planning, not only to provide professional assistance to Atlanta couples, but also to embrace inclusion and deliver the best client experience around.

**Mitchell Event Planning**

**Website**
MitchellEventPlanning.com

**Phone**
404-919-7224

**Email**
matt@mitchelleventplanning.com

**Instagram**
Instagram.com/MitchellEventPlanning

**Facebook**
Facebook.com/MitchellEventPlanning

**Yelp**
Yelp.com/biz/Mitchell-Event-Planning-Atlanta

**Pinterest**
Pinterest.com/MitchellEventPlanning

# The Code Queen

They call her "The Code Queen," a name befitting her expertise and celebrity on YouTube where Nayeli Gómez unlocks the mysteries of writing code specifically for the cloud-based web design platform, Wix. It all started eight years ago with a Google search on how to make money from home after she found herself both unexpectedly pregnant and unemployed. The top result, "Web Design," prompted her second search, "How to make a free website." Despite her father's objection that it would be too complicated, Nayeli became a web designer.

Since then, she's achieved many milestones: Wix Ambassador for Rio Grande Valley (in McAllen Texas), Wix Certified Trainer, Wix Certified Webmaster, Wix Design Expert, Wix Arena Pro Designer, Wix Alpha Tester, Wix Beta Tester and Wix Code Expert. Her website design talent is in demand to create the best online presence for a broad range of businesses.

Nayeli was given the opportunity to learn Wix Code before it was released as a Beta test. She enjoys making Wix Code training tutorials on YouTube. Up to fifteen people a day subscribe to her channel, which currently has over 1,100 subscribers. They've watched over 4,500 hours of her videos. 'How to Create a Custom Private Client Member Dashboard,' is the most popular one with almost 14,000 views. Nayeli, a Council Member on the Wix Community YouTube channel, also started the "Totally Codable" community Facebook group.

# Conversation with Nayeli Gómez

*What inspired you to train Wix users how to learn code?*

**Nayeli Gómez:** I was fortunate enough to be part of the Alpha testing group, which basically means I was able to test out the Wix Code product way before anybody even knew that Wix was working on it. So, we signed a non-disclosure and I tested it out. I fell in love with it right away. Immediately. The first day, I completed all the tutorial videos that they had at that time. I went inside the editor. I started playing around with Wix Code and I absolutely loved it. I had a really hard time not saying anything about this amazing feature that I had been testing in secret for weeks. It was a lot of pressure.

Finally, there came a day when they announced it to everybody, the release of Wix Code! That was an amazing day. I was so happy, because at that moment I was finally able to share my love and enthusiasm for Wix Code. What happened though, was everybody heard the word "code..." and they freaked out. They *didn't* love it. They rejected it, they were mad even, and that made me feel sad. I could not believe that nobody saw what I saw. I couldn't believe that it wasn't accepted the way that I thought it would be. I really thought it was world-changing. Databases! It is just amazing to be able to have them on a website, and on top of that, on a *Wix* website so you can design it easily. I was excited, I was happy, and basically my bubble burst when everybody didn't receive it the same. So, I thought, "You know what? It's OK."

I thought, "They're only reacting this way because they haven't really seen it in action." So, I got on my computer and got into the editor. I'm not shy, so I recorded myself and walked them through the steps. I *showed them* what Wix Code really does and how easy it is. I recorded my first video, a real long video, about forty-five minutes long. I was on a mission to show everybody, "Hey, look at this. It is so easy, and I know you're gonna love it too." I was the only one that had an actual code video. I was surprised at how many people watched it. *All* of it, until the end!

So, from that one video, people would send requests, "Hey, but I don't know how to do *this.* Can you show me how to do that?" I made another video and another video and another video, and that's how I started to do my Wix Code videos to teach people.

Because people wanted to *know* more, I wanted to *learn* more, *and* I wanted to show them that I was learning with them at the same time, with the same exact access to the resources that Wix developers were coming out with: the Wix code forum, the tutorial videos that they had, the articles, everything. I made it a mission to teach everyone how to use all these things, to do the wonderful things that were in my head or that other people wanted to do that were in *their* heads. I wanted to make it possible for them. I started as a non-coder, I had zero experience. For me to push through that barrier and show them, "Hey, look at me. You're literally seeing me live learning here right now, with you, and if I can do it, then you can do it too."

*Can you share a lesson you learned early on, that still impacts how you do business today?*

**Nayeli Gómez:** Well that's a good question. I learned that I apparently don't have time to answer everyone's questions.

People see me now as a source, a person they can trust to get the answers or the direction that they need to find those answers. I don't have enough time in the day to help everyone. Because of that, I created a Facebook group for questions, so everybody can kind of help and share their thoughts or insights on how to do something.

I am now being booked two, even three months ahead of time. I had to make it a rule if you don't book my services ahead of time, I just cannot be on-demand to help you. It was a real hard rule to put into place, but I stick to that rule. Even though I try to be real active in my group, in replying to literally hundreds of emails that I get every day, every hour even, and all the messages that I get on YouTube, I had to learn how to organize that. I learned it was necessary to make sure that I was able to cover everything and help everyone as much as I could.

*Tell us about Totally Codable and how you are helping your clients.*

**Nayeli Gómez:** Well, Totally Codable is a website. I decided to make a brand dedicated specifically to code-to learn Wix Code snippets, to watch Wix Code tutorials, to purchase Wix Code templates, even get free Wix codes.

I wanted to make it a real nice organized place that was easy to understand and easy to retrieve whatever information you needed about whatever project you were trying to work on. I've also included "Featured Coders" and "Featured Designers" who are actual Wix experts that I personally know or have taught or have seen accomplish high levels of either design or Wix coding. They are professionals I can recommend to others because again, I am not always available, and you shouldn't have to Google somebody randomly for help. I wanted to give my expert recommendation to these expert coders and designers and kind of highlight them. That way, the community can go to these people because they know Wix, Wix Code and they can probably help you with whatever you need.

People come to Totally Codable to find the "Code Queen." That's who I am. That's what I'm known as. People come to me if they have a problem. Maybe they just need advice on what their current website looks like, maybe they don't even know where to start, or how to continue what they started. People come to me to find a solution.

I am good at what I do because I think logically. I speak the logic language. Everybody has a different level of web design knowledge or code knowledge. Everybody has a different vocabulary. Everybody explains things in a different way. I can decipher what you're telling me, understand what you're trying to accomplish, and then I can speak your language and explain to you what you need to know or learn or the steps you need to take to accomplish exactly that. I have people, clients, students all over the world speaking all different languages. English is probably not their first language, which is completely fine because I can help every single person. Even if you've never made a website before. Even if this is your fifth or tenth website. I can guarantee that I can point you in the right direction and help you solve your problems in the most efficient way possible.

*What do you feel are the biggest myths out there when it comes to learning Wix Code?*

**Nayeli Gómez:** One of the myths that you hear is: because it has the word "code" in it, you're going to be dealing with a whole bunch of numbers and letters and symbols and encoding stuff. That's not entirely accurate. While you can add custom code on different things, the majority of Wix code is just configuring settings. You click a button, you turn something on, you click another button, you tell it to point somewhere else. It's basically just clicking a bunch of buttons on the screen. Wix Code is not entirely one hundred percent actual code writing.

Another myth is that people think that if you "get" javascript, and because Wix Code speaks in the javascript language, then all you do is copy paste and you're done. That is also not true. There are Wix APIs. There are some reference articles and good material for you to learn how to tweak your code before you copy and paste it into your website page. It needs to speak the Wix Code language. It's not simply javascript, it's Wix Code, a little hybrid, its own language. It's pretty neat.

*What are some of the most common fears about learning Wix Code and how can people get past them?*

**Nayeli Gómez:** All I can say is don't be afraid! Don't be afraid to learn to code and if you do want to try it out, I recommend you go to YouTube. Watch my hover effect Wix code video. That is the shortest video. It's only about ten, fifteen minutes long. It will show you the quickest way to learn actual code, to tweak code writing. It covers a lot of different things in a short amount of time. It's easy to do.

Try it. Make a copy of your current website or get a blank template. Don't be afraid to break something. I mean, how much can you break? There's always the back button, but all I can say is just try it.

*What other perceived obstacles do you see that might be preventing Wix users from seeking the help of a code trainer?*

**Nayeli Gómez:** I think that possibly users may be afraid to reach out to someone because they don't know the code language or advanced vocabulary words, which you should not need to worry about. Find someone, for example, in a group, maybe Facebook. There's a lot of Facebook groups that you can join and just ask a question. Slowly you will feel comfortable about talking code, and then it will be easy to ask for help later. Just ask them, "Hey, since you're answering my questions, do you offer training as a service or could you possibly show me how to do this?"

*What are three advantages of learning Wix Code?*

**Nayeli Gómez:** I think the three best advantages to learning how to code are: One, you will be able to enter a new realm of possibilities. You can create that custom form that you really wanted. It breaks design barriers. That's a good thing.

Two, it can save you money. Perhaps there's a specific app that you really want because of a specific function, let's say to capture information of your website visitors, store that information somewhere, and provide a link to somewhere else. Something like that. Well, if you learn how to build it from scratch with Wix Code, you'll save that money and you can use it towards something else, maybe towards some Wix Code training classes so you can learn more advanced stuff.

I think the third one is you will feel accomplished. You will feel like you've reached another level of web design skill or your coding skill. It's something that you should be very proud of and you can also show off. People will see your website with all the fancy stuff. They'll like it and *want* to be there.

*What are some of the little-known pitfalls or common mistakes you see Wix users make on the road to learning Wix Code?*

**Nayeli Gómez:** It's so funny, because the smallest things, the smallest mistakes, the most common ones are the ones that can have you sit in front of your computer for hours, sometimes even days, when it was the tiniest little thing. I recommend you check the spelling. One letter, just one letter will break the entire code.

It is also case-sensitive. One capital letter that shouldn't be capitalized could also break your code. If you do happen to make these small mistakes, just take a break, take a breather. It's good to have another pair of fresh eyes look at it, so maybe even post your question in a group, whether it be the code forum or the Facebook group. Learn from your mistake. Remember what the problem was and how it was fixed. Don't rely on somebody else to just fix it for you. And then you continue and move on.

*Can you share an example of how you have helped your clients overcome these obstacles and succeed in learn Wix Code?*

**Nayeli Gómez:** I help a lot of my clients mostly by personalized consultations or training sessions. I do a lot of interactive consulting using screen shares. I know how to teach, basically. If I walk you through each step personally, you're able to absorb that information a lot better, especially if I'm using a site that you see every day, not a random made up training site. I think it's more valuable when we're looking at your site and learning on your website.

*What's the most important question Wix users should ask themselves as they consider learning Wix Code?*

**Nayeli Gómez:** If you are considering learning Wix Code, I think you should ask yourself what the reason is for wanting to learn. Is it for your own personal benefit for your own website? Is it to teach others how to do the same thing? Is it to grow your business? Are you trying to offer services that other designers don't offer? First, think about what your true intentions are of learning code. That will help you plan.

*What's the most important thing Wix users should consider when evaluating a trainer?*

**Nayeli Gómez:** If you are considering hiring a trainer, make sure that they are knowledgeable and that *they* will be the one training you. Some people hire other people to do the training. Try to speak to the actual person that will be training you. Don't ask for examples of codes that they've done. That does not prove anything. All it proves is that they knew how to find a code and show it to you. Ask questions, like, "What do you recommend for this and this and this?" to help you determine if the person is qualified or not. You can also ask for references and check out their reviews. Find out what their experience was. That way, you can make an informed decision on whether you want to work with that person. Before you purchase a whole bunch of hours with that person, maybe purchase the smallest time available, whether that be fifteen minutes, twenty minutes, thirty minutes or an hour. Purchase the smallest time available so you can see if you're comfortable working with them. If you learn from them and accomplish what you wanted to accomplish, you'll know they are the right person for you.

*How can someone find out more about Nayeli Gómez, Totally Codable and how you can help?*

**Nayeli Gómez:** You can search for my Totally Codable group on Facebook. In that group, you can post questions, ask for guidance, ask for advice, or even just show off what you've done with Wix Code. It's a group dedicated to Wix Code only. If you would like personalized consultation or training by me, simply visit my website, TotallyCodable.com. Scroll all the way to the bottom and click on "Contact Code Queen." It'll send me an email and I'll get your message. That way we can go over any questions you may have regarding training or consultation services with me.

## About Nayeli Gómez

Nayeli Gómez, also known as Code Queen Nayeli, is an accomplished web designer with a passion for teaching. A pioneer in the use of Wix Code, Nayeli created the Totally Codable brand to showcase not only her expertise, but that of other web design professionals and coders. She has a global audience of subscribers on YouTube and conducts in-person workshops for the first and only Wix web design community in South Texas serving the Rio Grande Valley. When she's not designing, consulting or teaching, Nayeli can be found riding a bicycle or spending time with her daughter and family. Here is how to contact Nayeli:

**Website**
TotallyCodable.com

**Email**
nayeli@totallycodable.com

**YouTube**
YouTube.com/c/WixExpert

**Facebook**
Facebook.com/CodeQueen

# Protecting and Nourishing
# Skin for Life™

Millions of people suffer emotionally, physically and financially daily combating skin care issues revolving around dryness, erythema, inflammation, pain, and infection. Current treatments are often ineffective, expensive, and/or damaging to the skin with long-term use.

Julie A. Stein is the CEO and Founder of DermaHealth Science, a company based in Alpharetta, Ga, devoted to providing quality, non-synthetic topical supplements to address the very same issues stated above. Their focus is on improving skin health from a Corneotherapy approach which supports the innate immune system and establishes a healthy skin barrier for protection against environmental toxins, harmful microbes and UV rays. Their topicals are scientifically designed to supply the necessary nutritive ingredients for improving and facilitating cellular function. As a result, skin texture, moisture content, integrity and overall health and appearance of skin is improved.

# Conversation with Julie A. Stein

*Tell us a little bit about yourself and your background. Also, what is the typical client that you are going to help with DermaHealth Science?*

**Julie A. Stein**: I have a Master's in Physical Therapy and practiced for thirteen years with the last three specializing in wound care and acute care at a local children's hospital in Atlanta. I fell in love with healing wounds and the care involved with preventing, treating and lessening pain.

In 2007, I ventured into becoming an entrepreneur full-time. As a single mother of two children, I didn't want to be limited by working for someone. It's now 18 years later, and I still feel it was one of the best decisions I've made. The variety of experiences, growth, and life-lessons has allowed me to do what I'm doing today.

This current journey started about five years ago when I looked in the mirror and noticed I was looking older. Like most women, I went shopping for the "miracle cream" but, unfortunately, didn't get the results desired, or the products were too expensive to even try. Bound and determined to look younger, I began experimenting with natural ingredients like Coconut Oil and Shea Butter, and liked the results. I said to myself, "Maybe this is what I'm supposed to be doing. Maybe I should be diving in and developing a skin care product for people because surely I'm not the only frustrated one." So, I did. I had to start from square one, learning about what causes skin to breakdown and age, what causes dry vs. oily skin, and learn about the 'good, bad, and ugly' ingredients available. It was important that the product be above average, meaning not something anyone would think to develop on their own as well as truly address the issues at hand. I wanted to merge nature with science and develop a non-synthetic solution for skin health and protection. That's how DermaHealth Science began.

The typical client is someone who's truly interested in the health of their skin to achieve optimal appearance, rather than just achieving healthy-feeling skin through traditional cosmetics.

*The skin care market is certainly massive. Who are your primary clients? In your introduction, you were talking about healing the skin. Is that healing from scars or is that just from having bad skin and trying to make it look better?*

**Julie A. Stein**: We focus on the health of the skin and facilitating the cells' natural functions. Scarred tissue is already healed, although the appearance can fade overtime for many individuals. Legally, we cannot label this product as a treatment. However, the ingredients selected are key components involved in the skin's cellular function, and they are combined at specific quantities to enhance absorption and efficacy. So, we improve the skin's appearance by improving its health. Synthetic products can make your skin feel healthy and soft because they coat the surface with silicon-based ingredients and temporarily trap moisture for added firmness, but when that moisture evaporates, the skin resumes its previous appearance. That's why moisturizers are limited in how long they work; the water content evaporates over a period of several hours.

Our clients are anyone that wants healthy skin, but typically the clients are women anywhere in the range of 20s to mid-50s. I've had teenagers and older women use it and love it, but 20s to 50s is most common. Recently, middle-aged men have been trying it with excellent outcomes as well.

*What is the base of the product?*

**Julie A. Stein**: It is an oil-based product without water, which means there are no potentially allergenic preservatives or need for emulsifiers that ultimately cause the loss of the skin's natural oils. It contains the necessary omega fatty acids, antioxidants, and natural anti-inflammatories that support optimal skin cell development and water retention. All skin types benefit from this product, even oily skin.

*Is the product called DermaHealth Science? Or is that your company and this is one of the products? I know you are officially launching later this year.*

**Julie A. Stein**: DermaHealth Science is the company name. We are likely going to go with the name ProHealth pH. It certainly is descriptive of the product.

*How is ProHealth pH going to help with dry skin?*

**Julie A. Stein**: Someone with dry skin has an alkaline pH higher than 7.0. Healthy pH is around 5.5. Dry skin is compromised skin and can more easily become infected. For example, people with eczema have dry, itchy skin. Bacteria that don't normally pose a problem, enter the skin of these people and cause further damage and inflammation. Dry skin is something that should not be ignored.

*So how long does it take to start seeing a difference using ProHealth pH?*

**Julie A. Stein**: The earliest we have seen is about three days but typically within five to seven days. We're noticing the results are lasting more than 24 hours. The longer it's used, the healthier the skin becomes so the effects last longer.

*What are some of the misconceptions people have about skin care? There are thousands of products out there on the market. How does someone choose the one that's right for them and healthy for them?*

**Julie A. Stein**: There are many products in the market with lots of marketing. You really must read closely to make sure that you are getting what you believe you are purchasing. Cosmetics are a "temporary alteration in the appearance of the skin". They are not designed to eliminate your wrinkles. What they do is improve the moisture content on the surface of your skin so the wrinkles are less noticeable. Cosmetics do not actually improve the collagen content so, again, read the labeling carefully so you don't overpay for what you expect.

Another misconception is that coconut oil won't clog your pores. It's all over the Internet. Unfortunately, it has a four out of five rating for being a 'pore-clogging ingredient'.

A favorite misconception of mine is to keep your skin slightly wet after showering and then apply lotion to trap the moisture. The top of your skin contains an oil emulsion so that water internally is less likely to evaporate. Water on the surface will not be absorbed into the skin for this reason. The only water that can benefit the actual hydration of skin is the water you drink. Not surface water. That merely evaporates. Anyway, water is needed for proper cellular function so focus more on drinking rather than trapping.

*What kind of natural products are in ProHealth pH, and how do they help your skin?*

**Julie A. Stein**: The natural ingredients that we focus on are omega fatty acids. Certain omega fatty acids cannot be synthesized by the body so they must be consumed. We have taken those same fatty acids for an 'outside-in' approach to skin nutrition. These fatty acids are vital for cellular performance and, ultimately, the skin's ability to ward off infection and maintain a healthy appearance. We also use antioxidants, which help not only with maintaining the 'life' of the product, but to aid in preventing breakdown of the skin from UV rays, pollution, and eating poorly. Lastly, anti-inflammatories also aid in protection and discourage breakdown. When these components come together in the right quantities, the skin is in a state of homeostasis with a pH level vital for promoting the life of healthy bacteria and an intact innate immune system.

In a nutshell, we address both cause and symptoms to reach healthy skin. Many products on the market merely focus on the symptoms.

*As far as helping with conditions such as acne, do you have a solution for that?*

**Julie A. Stein**: With acne, you have inflammation and often excess oil, which ProHealth pH does show to address. We have done beta testing on teens and myself personally.

The results were great improvement. It's important to note that many acne cleansers strip the skin of its oils and are at a pH that promotes dry skin. The oil content is viewed as the culprit for acne. This is not the case. Their skin is in a compromised state so it's important to focus on the pH and skin barrier health, not on stripping the oils. When the skin barrier is healthy, the oil is no longer a problem. This is the result we're seeing with our product.

*As far as having an oil-based product and putting it on already oily skin, how does that work?*

**Julie A. Stein**: Some people get nervous about using an oil-based product when they have naturally oily skin. The particular oils used in ProHealth pH absorb quickly, and help to improve the skin's pH. When the pH is in a normal range, the oil content on the face has been reduced.

*What's the secret to having fresh, healthy skin? If it came down to just one thing that you can do or to put on your skin, what would that be and how does it help so much?*

**Julie A. Stein**: To say one specific thing is hard, but the omega fatty acids are very important. It's also very important to not exfoliate more than 1x/week and not with harsh abrasives. In fact, gently rubbing the face once over with a washcloth is all that is really needed. Also, when choosing a cleanser, make sure the pH is no more than 7.0. Many cleansers for acne are around 8.5 which will dry the skin and further exacerbate symptoms.

As far as what to avoid, make sure your products don't contain perfumes, coloring, mineral oil, silicone or silicone-based ingredients like dimethicone, petrolatum, EDTA or PEGs, which stands for polyethylene glycol and is often followed by a number. This last ingredient will cause the Washout Effect. It will literally emulsify water on your skin with the natural oils, pulling them out and causing chronic dryness. These are some of the main ingredients to avoid, anyway.

I guess that was a bit more than 'one.' Skin is complicated.

*ProHealth pH sounds like a great product. When will DermaHealth Science get this product to market?*

**Julie A. Stein**: We are getting very close. Several tests need to be completed first. Depending on funding, it may not be until late 2nd or 3rd quarter. We have a nice pool of people who've tested this product and are repeat customers. If you have interest in trying it, we are currently offering a one-time free sample and provide larger amounts for purchase.

*Do you have a specific case study? What condition did they have and what were the results of ProHealth pH?*

**Julie A. Stein**: People with eczema have very dry skin and I have a client that wanted to try it. I gave her ProHealth pH, and it cleared up her eczema. I am not going to attribute it to treating the eczema, but it helped with the dryness of her skin and helped with the irritation. In doing so, her eczema cleared up. The skin became healthy because it received the necessary nutrients.

*What inspired you to become an entrepreneur and bring a product to market?*

**Julie A. Stein**: I have always been a little creative, but the trigger that released my entrepreneur-self was an incident that happened when bathing my six-month-old son. He was in an infant bath seat and it literally tipped over. Thank Heavens I was right there and was able to pull him out. That experience started the whole process of inventing products that will help others. I found a patent attorney and got started on learning what it takes to be an entrepreneur and take a product to market. While the infant bath seat did receive two patents, and another couple other ideas I had also got patented, I've not yet formally brought a product to market. DermaHealth Science is making this dream come true.

*Is there anything else you are doing with the product?*

**Julie A. Stein**: I have a couple formulations underway for medical applications to reduce nosocomial infections brought on by Staph aureus. We're at the initial stages of testing efficacy for eradication of this bacteria and will move on to test for MRSA.

*How do we get in contact with Julie Stein to find out more?*

**Julie A. Stein**: You can either find me on LinkedIn and message me there, or you can email me at dermahealthscience @gmail.com. I also have a Twitter account @DermaInsight if you'd like more information regarding skin health.

# About Julie Stein

Julie Stein is known for her motivation, high energy, and fearless drive to reach goals both personally and professionally. She excels in innovation (recipient of four patents), B2B connecting/relationship building, and problem solving. Her latest invention evolves from a culmination of her knowledge and experience in wound care with extensive research in inflammation and pathophysiology of skin. These topical products are on target to improve the lives of people worldwide, both physiologically and emotionally.

Having no regrets in her life, Julie's a firm believer that everything happens for a reason and that something positive can be found in every situation. She's enjoying life's journey and creating every day, week, month and year to produce the results desired for her and her family.

Julie has a Masters in Physical Therapy from Washington University School of Medicine, Phi Beta Kappa member and Magna Cum Laude from Luther College in Decorah, IA. She currently resides in Alpharetta, GA and is enjoying watching her two children become young adults and learn what life is truly about.

**LinkedIn**
LinkedIn.com/in/SteinJulieA

**Twitter**
@DermaInsight

**Email**
DermaHealthScience@gmail.com

At DermaHealth Science, we provide gentle, nutritive topical products to enhance skin health and aid in protecting against toxins, harmful bacteria and UV rays.

*Please read the following Medical Disclaimer:*

* Content is provided for general informational purposes and should not be considered medical advice. Product information is not intended to diagnose, treat, cure or prevent any disease. This information has not been evaluated or approved by the Food & Drug Administration.

* Comments and feedback about product effectiveness are based on customer, staff, and family opinions. Individual results may vary.

* DermaHealth Science is not liable for any individual reaction to any particular ingredient. Remember to read our labels and ingredient lists carefully and follow the appropriate directions for use. While each ingredient has been selected for its nutritive benefits and high tolerance, those with sensitivity or allergy issues should consult with their dermatologist before using. An allergy patch test is recommended if there is any doubt or history of skin reactions. Discontinue use if a reaction occurs.

* Please consult a healthcare provider if you have any questions about a particular health condition.

# Overcoming Fear Fatigue

Are you exhausted watching others pass you by in life? Are your dreams on the shelf because you've been doing the safe thing for years?

Lorri Silvera is a life and business coach who helps Christian women in the marketplace survive and thrive. She has worked with a #1 New York Times best-selling author, elected officials, hospitality companies, and entrepreneurs helping them develop their message, gain exposure, and grow their business.

Through her work, she has seen women debilitated by and completely fatigued by fear. She believes that many of us are living half-lived lives. That we are so wrapped up in our own fears, often without even knowing it, and it's holding us back from living fulfilled and having joy, peace, and contentment.

In this interview, Lorri Silvera shares some of the psychology behind fear and practical steps that you can take to stop it dead in its tracks and start living the life you desire!

## Conversation with Lorri Silvera

*What do you see as the biggest obstacle holding people back from achieving their dreams?*

**Lorri Silvera:** Fear. Fear is the number one killer of all dreams. People are so bound up by fear they don't even recognize it any more. We often disguise fear as other things and even wear it as a badge of honor in some cases. Worry, concern, and perfectionism are rooted in fear.

Don Miguel Ruiz, in his book *The Four Agreements: A Practical Guide to Personal Freedom* states that all emotions are rooted in only two – love and fear. 1 John 4:18 says, "There is no fear in love. But perfect love drives out fear, because fear has to do with punishment. The one who fears is not made perfect in love."

Fear is actually not our highest or best state of mind or being. James 1:17 says, "For God has not given us the spirit of fear; but of power, and of love, and of a sound mind."

Fear is really not as big of a mystery as people make it out to be. Psychologically, when you have never done something before, your brain doesn't know how to react. Because your brain doesn't know what to expect, it goes into protection mode and tries to keep you from doing anything that might harm you.

I love what Gay Hendricks says, "Fear is excitement without breath."

The other interesting about fear is that it's completely irrational. Think about it. What is the statistical probability that your son or daughter died in a car accident because they're five minutes late? Slim to none. But our brain really creates all of these worst-case scenarios, and once we follow that trail mentally our emotions kick in and our state of mind goes downhill from there!

Fear really doesn't have any new tactics. It's always the same thing over and over again. It's exhausting! It's fatiguing.

Fill in the blank on this sentence, "If it weren't for _____, I would be doing what I dream about doing."

Did the word you put in the space have anything to do with fear at its roots? It's likely.

The great news about fear is that you can overcome it! We'll save my tips for overcoming fear until the end.

*It's interesting that you say perfectionism is rooted in fear. Can you tell us a little more about that?*

**Lorri Silvera:** What I realized, as a recovering perfectionist myself, is that my idea of things needing to be *just so* was holding me back from really living all out. It can show up in things like the fear of being seen, the fear of being judged, and hiding.

This is a really terrible state of being. Our dreams, words, and desires are meant to be expressed. When we hold back, it starts to take a toll on physically, mentally and emotionally.

My clients will often say something to the effect of, "Someone is already doing what I want to do so I can't do it. I have to find something else." To that I say – rubbish!

Look at all the hamburger restaurants. Look at all the pizza franchises. Look around. The universe is abundant.

Nothing we do on earth will ever be perfect, so we should stop trying. Done is better than perfect!

When it comes to creating a business that may be similar to someone else's, the difference between you and someone else is your story and life experience. Your story is what will bring a unique perspective to your work. Just like no one else has your fingerprints, no one else has your story.

By sharing your story, you can bring life and new perspectives to people. Just the other day, a colleague shared that her dream was to live in Paris. She owns her own business, so I responded that she could consider working remotely for a few weeks out of the year and after that a month and after that a few months. She had never thought of that before! We don't know what we don't know, and she probably thought it had to be all or nothing.

That's another big sign of perfectionism. It breeds extremism. This idea of all or nothing is really destructive and keeps us from enjoying life. I was watching a spiritual leader on YouTube who was talking about being more aware of the life around us. If you're all wrapped up in what you did or didn't do and what you can or can't do, are you observing the beauty of your surroundings? Doubtful.

Being able to appreciate your blessings will take you to a whole new level in your life and business!

*How else does fear impact us?*

**Lorri Silvera:** Fear has so many other negative side effects. Fear and stress are closely related.

Have you ever been in a situation where your fight or flight response kicked in? Your body goes into a state of stress. I recently learned it takes hours for you to recover from that stress response. Sorry, but I'm not going to allow that person who is not worth it to me anymore to get me bent out of shape and take up hours of my life recovering!

Negative emotions have energy associated with them and if you don't express them they'll get stored in your body. Have you ever been so angry you want to punch something? Emotions are energy and if you don't deal with them, they'll build up. You'll start to feel aches and pains that weren't there before.

You can work through negative emotions by releasing them. This can be done through physical activity, journaling, and other methods. I've enjoyed a few boxing classes and have a handful of journals with some hard times that I've been through.

Fear can also impact your confidence level. You can begin to experience self-doubt and self-sabotage. When you don't feel secure and are guided by fear, instead of the higher emotion of love, you won't make good decisions.

Fear acts like a blinder and doesn't allow us to see the bigger picture. It limits our perspective.

If fear is preventing you from taking action, simply go back to your why. Why do you want to do this? Why is this important to you?

For example, your why is probably connected with your family. Maybe you dream of starting a business but are afraid to take the risk because you have a steady paycheck.

If you want to overcome fear and give your boss your two weeks' notice, start to visualize yourself on the other side. That's right. Take a moment to picture yourself doing what it is what you would love to do. This again will help you to re-train your brain. If you see yourself as already having what you want or doing what you want, it will become more believable for you.

Picture yourself at your home office. Picture yourself picking your children up from school every day. Imagine going on a family vacation and not having to answer emails or text messages from the office.

You can also write a personal mission statement. This will help you ground back into your why. It's a more concise version of your why. My mission statement is that I help Christian women survive and thrive in the marketplace.

*How does someone overcome fear and put it to rest?*

**Lorri Silvera:** I love this question! The principles will be the same for everyone, but the execution will likely be different. There are three things that I recommend to overcome fear fatigue.

The first thing is to recognize fear for what it is – irrational, illogical and just your brain's way to keep you safe. Now that you have a better understanding of fear after reading this book, you can stop the emotional getaway train dead in its tracks!

The second thing is to develop some practices that you implement immediately when you feel fear coming up. It could be deep breathing, taking a quick walk, or journaling. Whatever your method, you've got to pattern interrupt what's going on. Don't just keep thinking about it. STOP! Re-set.

You can also add in positive affirmations to your routine. If you're afraid of losing your job, for example, you might develop a few things that you say out loud such as:

I'm always in the right place at the right time.
God knows what's best for me and has a plan for my life.
I'm excited for whatever God has next!

Confessing positive words out loud helps to change the way your brain processes information. You might feel silly doing it at first, but giving voice to the words will help change your thought patterns, then your emotions, then your actions, and finally your results! It's calling things that don't currently exist into existence. Our words have creative power!

Romans 4:18 says, "God, who gives life to the dead, and calls the things that are not, as though they were."

The third thing is to regularly practice gratitude. Appreciating what we already have helps us to see what we are quick to overlook. I've never heard of someone on their deathbed saying they wished they could have attended more meetings at work. Their regrets are always the trips not taken, the time away from the family, and not saying "I love you" enough.

You absolutely can take hold of your thoughts and transform them so that you can experience life in a whole new way.

We were not designed to live in fear. We are created to live free and live out God's purpose for our lives. He doesn't desire us to be stuck and stagnant because we're afraid.

It's time for you to start living your life. Don't let anything get in the way of your dreams or desires. It's time to finally go for it!

# About Lorri Silvera

Lorri Silvera built her first six-figure business by age 32 and did it all wrong – she was a maxed out, stressed out, and burned out workaholic. After the near death of a family member, she reevaluated her life and realized that she wasn't doing what she was truly passionate about. Now she helps Christian women survive and thrive in the marketplace. She is driven to help women experience greater wealth, health, love and travel the world!

Her professional background includes working for a #1 New York Times best-selling author, political campaign management, and hospitality marketing. She and her husband make their home in Destin, Florida. Connect with her on social media.

**Website**
LorriSilvera.com

**Email**
Lorri@LorriSilvera.com

**Location**
Destin, Florida

**Facebook**
Facebook.com/LorriSilveraFan

**Twitter**
@LorriSilvera

**Other**
LinkedIn.com/in/Lorri-Silvera-80446932

# Helping Women Over 40 Look and Feel 15 Years Younger and Achieve a Pain-Free Life

Batista Gremaud is the co-founder of the International Institute of Body Design, helping busy women over 40 look and feel 15 years younger by eliminating aches and pains with Dr Fitness USA's proprietary system.

Batista started her professional journey at the age of three at her parent's academy of dance and dramatic arts in Switzerland. She made an international career as a ballet and flamenco artist and has performed all over the world. Her repertoire of over twenty-five choreographies includes ballet, dance/theater, public television performances, summer concert series and video productions.

When injuries ended her dancing career, Batista discovered the transformative power of Stephen Hercy's (Dr Fitness USA) body design prescription strength training system. Inspired by her success with the program, she helped design an online version for both men and women that can now help people all over the world. She is committed to helping as many women as possible to lose weight, increase their strength, and gain more confidence while enjoying a pain-free life.

# Conversation with Batista Gremaud

*To help our audience understand your perspective on fitness, can you tell us a little bit about your health and fitness journey and how it shaped your ability to help your clients achieve their goals?*

**Batista Gremaud:** I was a performer. I was a dancer of ballet first. When I was in my mid-20s, I broke my foot which terminated my ballet career, and then I recycled myself into a flamenco dancer.

That is what I did my entire life. I started when I was three, and I kept going until I turned 48, touring the world and doing everything in the dance community from having companies, to teaching. So that was my life. I was already very conscious of my health and my body because you must be when you are a dancer. Dancers must fit in the costumes, and so they always watch what they eat and what they do. However, after I turned 40, things started to change for me. My body began to change, and I think that is a normal thing at that age as the hormones start changing.

When I turned 40, whatever I was doing to keep myself fit just didn't work anymore. I had many injuries through dancing. The show must go on, so if you have pain or something happens, you must show up. By the time I was 45, I had every injury in the book. I had shoulder pain, back pain, neck pain, bad knees, Achilles. You name it; I had it. Not only that, but I started gaining weight. So that was not very pleasant. I was gaining almost a pound per month, so it was horrifying. With so many injuries and gaining weight as I did, I could not dance. So, I wondered, "How will I support myself?"

I am a long practitioner of meditation and positive thinking, and I believe in those types of things. I started putting it out there that I need a solution because I knew I had the power to manifest something that would turn my life around. Low and behold, the next day after making this huge intention, I was at Dr Fitness USA, totally by accident, which at this point it was not an accident, if you understand what I mean.

He told me about his system and how he works with women over 40. He told me never to do anything that is uncomfortable regarding exercise and fitness. I did not understand that at all because in dance we always did everything that was uncomfortable. We always pushed ourselves. We always did more. However, the conversation was so different and so unusual, and I had tried everything except that. That was completely new to me, and it was based on strength training and weightlifting. Because I was injured, just the thought of carrying something heavy was frightening to me. I did not know how that would help me with my injuries.

I decided that I was going to accept what was presented to me because I prayed for it. Sometimes we pray for something and expect it to look a certain way, but when it comes in our life it looks different. So, I decided to keep an open mind, and I jumped in. Within a couple of months, all my injuries disappeared. Within a couple of weeks, I stopped gaining weight. It was like a miracle. That was the beginning of this journey for me. I was so fascinated with the process that I began researching and studying, and I picked his brain day in and day out. I wanted to know everything, and that is how I ended up dating him, marrying him, and how we have a family business. It was a love story and the start of our business. I understand what women go through at that age; I have gone through it, and I am a product of the product, so I have first-hand experience.

*Although you do train men, you specialize in training women over 40 who usually don't have time, who are starting the hormonal experience associated with weight gain and loss of energy, many of them have like you did, are experiencing some kinds of injury or pain. My question is, why do you focus on this group and why are they so attracted to working with you?*

**Batista Gremaud:** I focus on this group because I have the first-hand experience. I can relate. I have the empathy and the sympathy. It was my journey, so I have an affinity with that age group and the problems associated with it. It works because I walked through the journey myself. I feel very confident that when I work with women at that age group that I really can make a difference in their lives because I know the ins and outs of what's going on. I do train men as well, but with them, it is a different story. With men, we are talking about testosterone and different issues that I have not experienced myself. So even though I know intellectually how to work with men, I do not have the practical experience to have gone through that. My husband, Stephen, works very well with men, so we make a good team.

*I know that many of your clients have tried programs before and they failed. You have said that your program is often the last house on the block. How do you help clients overcome this fear and get back in the saddle, so they can start reaching their fitness goals?*

**Batista Gremaud:**  Yes, exactly. It has a lot to do with mindset because when you are in pain, you feel like it is the end of the world and it is very scary. The first thing that we must work with is the mindset. We can guide the person to look towards what is possible. For me, it works well because I walked the journey. I am a regular person. I am not a supermodel; I am not excessively muscular. When I talk to a woman, she can look at me and relate, and she can feel like "If she did it, I can do it."

There are many misconceptions and myths about fitness that women believe that hold them back. For example, walk into a gym and see what women do in the gym. Many women in the gym are just using treadmills.

They have the idea that if they do lots of aerobics, then they are going to lose weight. They are moving, but they are not going to get the fitness results that they think they are going to get. So that is the first misconception. A woman 40 and up really needs to focus on doing less aerobic and more strength training, and there are very specific reasons for that.

When you are on the treadmill or doing any aerobics, any type of Zumba or dance, you burn calories while you are doing the exercise. That's great, but when you do strength training, you burn calories while you are doing strength training and you continue to burn calories 72 hours after completing the workout. So, from a weight loss perspective, strength training gives you more results for the time spent.

There are other reasons. Excessive aerobic activities put considerable stress on the body. It produces inflammation, and inflammation produces cortisol, and cortisol is stress. Most women are already stressed in taking care of family and job obligations, so it is stress, stress, stress, stress, stress. Whether it is psychological or physical stress, at the end of the day it produces the same result. It produces inflammation, pain, and illness. When you go into your fitness activity, you want to try to reduce the stress so that you can have a place of comfort to heal the body. This is one of the reasons that we teach women never to do anything that is uncomfortable because if it is uncomfortable, then it is probably, in the long run, going to be harmful.

It does not mean that the workouts need to be easy or that they are not challenging. What we focus on is maximizing the power of the exercise so that the machine ergonomically supports your body, and the body is completely comfortable so that now you can maximize the potency of the exercise. When we talk about lifting weights for women, it brings us to another very big misconception. Which is the notion that they need to use very little weight and a lot of high reps.

*Why is that not the solution they are looking for?*

**Batista Gremaud:** Because that is also considered an aerobic type of activity. You see there are different muscle fibers in the body. When you do aerobic activity, high reps, low weight, running, treadmills and all this, they are considered aerobic activity, and it uses certain muscle fibers in the body. Strength training is a category of its own and uses different muscle fibers, so if the woman wants to rebuild muscle mass, then she needs to do strength training, not aerobic. We start losing muscle mass at age 30. So, it starts very early on. If the person does not do any strength training to maintain or rebuild the muscle mass, by the time the woman is 40 years old, she has lost a lot muscle. By the time she is 50, it is tremendous. People do not associate the problems they are having at that age with the muscle loss syndrome.

Suddenly the person has bad posture, and they are losing bone mass. When they start having bad posture it causes more problems, causes stagnation in the body. When you have stagnation, you have an illness like arthritis; now you have back pain. Now you have all kinds of problems.

That is the misconception. Women over 40 need to do less aerobics and more strength training. When we talk about strength training, we talk about lifting a weight that's more than what most women do, which is five or ten pounds.

*Because you shared a considerable amount of good information, let me see if I can summarize some of the things that I heard.*

*One is, aerobic exercise is not necessarily bad because it does keep you moving. It is burning calories, but it is not building muscle. As we age, we tend to lose muscle. So, people could weigh the same amount at 50 that they did at 20, but look terrible because they have lost, let's say 20 pounds of muscle, that has been replaced by fat.*

**Batista Gremaud:** Yes, we call that the skinny fat.

*If you have more muscle in your body, you will burn more calories just sitting around. As you build more muscle, your body will burn more calories, and your body functions more efficiently.*

*You also said that many women have the misconception that they must use light weights because they feel they cannot lift heavier weights. However, to get results, they must use a heavy enough weight to cause the muscles to want to grow. Could you talk about why it is important to lift heavier weights and what it takes to cause the response you want in the muscle to get the results?*

**Batista Gremaud:** Every person has a different target weight. It is not just about lifting more weight. Dr Fitness USA's genius is that he can pinpoint the correct weight for each person and each exercise based on what the person needs.

Another important thing to address is sequence. I see many people in the gyms, and I look at what they do, and there's no logical sequencing to what they do for exercise. What I learned through my research in the last ten years and what people do not realize is that strength training is a specific sport and that it requires a specific system.

Unlike martial arts or dancing, there is no system for strength training. I was a dancer, so I will relate to dancing for example. When you first start learning ballet, you learn that you need to do this exercise first, then the next one, then the next one. Everything is progressive, and will build upon each other so that at the end you will be a good dancer and you will have more roles.

It is also like martial arts. A good teacher will take you through the first step, the second step, and then you are going to get a white belt and then the yellow belt, green belt, whatever are the colors of the belts are. People do not realize that it is similar in strength training. It is a free for all, and personal trainers do not learn this in personal training school. I know because I did become a personal trainer.

Nobody has a system, and so this is what we have that is different from what's out there. Stephen, Dr Fitness USA, has put together a system, and he has been working on it for the last 55 years. He is 70 now, and he has been doing this since he was a teenager, so it has been a long, long, long track record, and it is specific. When you get into a gym, and you want to build strength, it is important to start by building from the ground up. We, for example, start with the leg press.

*Can you explain more about why you start there?*

**Batista Gremaud:**   Because your strength starts from the ground, it then propels the strength to the upper body. So, we can use how much weight the person is doing on the leg press to determine how much that person is going to be doing on a chest press because it is progressive.

It also has to do with the number of sets, the number of reps. So that you can build that strength and get the results that you want. A lot of women who use the treadmill or hike have very strong legs, but when you look at the upper body, it is completely undeveloped. It is like having two bodies in one person.

The idea is to rebuild the body from the inside out so that the upper body matches the lower body.

*When you are talking about matching the upper body with their lower body, you are not talking about turning women into bodybuilders, are you?*

**Batista Gremaud:** No. I am talking about having a symmetrically balanced physique.

*I am going to drill down a little bit regarding your workout. How can you get a good workout in 20 minutes?*

**Batista Gremaud:** You are referring to my tagline which is "We increase women's strength by 20 percent in 20 minutes." The workout is not 20 minutes; the workout is usually 40 minutes two to three times a week, but because it is like a prescription, it is a system, the strength will stay with you. The workout is not 20 minutes, the strength increase happens in the first 20 minutes though.

That is a little bit of a misconception. The strength increases in the first 20 minutes. Because of the progression of the exercises and the way the weight ranges and the set and the rep systems are designed, within the first 20 minutes of the workout, the person will immediately be stronger.

*How do you measure they are stronger?*

**Batista Gremaud:** It is very simple to measure because it is based on strength training. If the person comes in and they are leg pressing 40 pounds and in in the first 15 minutes or 20 minutes they went from 40 pounds to 70 pounds, that would be a 70 percent strength increase. So, when I say 20 percent, I am very conservative because we have women that go in and lift 20, 30 pounds on the leg press and within the first session, the first half an hour, the first 20 minutes they are at 190. I could even go and say 100 percent strength increase, but we do not want to, we keep is safe and feasible.

20 percent is very feasible, and it is very quantifiable because you are working with weights. I will give you an example.

We recently worked with a young woman who is 29 (we work with younger people too.) She has three kids and she has every autoimmune disorder that you can imagine. She cannot get out of bed.

She is in extreme pain all the time. We began working with her in our online program, so we never even physically went to the gym with her. We counseled her and suggested which gym she should join because not every gym is created equal. Some gyms look good, but the equipment is old and not conducive to a woman's success. The equipment is built more for a baseball player, a big tall man. So, that is another thing to take into consideration. You want to join a gym where they have some equipment you can use as a woman.

The first day she went to the gym, she leg-pressed five pounds. Okay, five pounds and I think the chest press she did not even manage to do it. We guided her through the process and within one week she was leg pressing 50 pounds and chest pressing 10 pounds.

We worked with her specifically for six weeks taking her through the whole process; now she is leg pressing 190 pounds and she's chest pressing 25-pound dumb bells (that was her target weight). She has no more pain, she is out of bed, she has her life back, and she is back at work doing what she loves to do.

*That is impressive not only in the gains that she made but also the outcomes. Most people work out because they want a different lifestyle or quality of life, not lifting 25-pound dumb bells. It is what does working out allow her to do, which is like you said, go back and do the things she wants to do.*

**Batista Gremaud:** That's it. Everybody wants to look good, but what we *really* want to have is energy. We want to be pain-free. We want to feel good. Especially after 40 and 50, we want to feel 15 years younger, and therefore we do it. Lifting with those specific weights and reps will give you results faster than anything else. That is why we do it.

*You mentioned that you help people select the right gym based on the equipment they have. You also make sure that people use the equipment properly to get the full impact from the exercise. Because if you exercise improperly on a machine, you are more apt to hurt yourself than get the results you want. Isn't that correct?*

**Batista Gremaud:** You got it. Exactly. When I started ten years ago, Stephen only worked with people one on one. People traveled from everywhere. They came to spend a week in Los Angeles, and they learned the program, and then they went back home, and they used the program. He has been doing this a long time. When I came along, I had a vision that we could expand and offer this to more people because women need it.

I spent eight years picking his brain and putting those programs online. Now we have programs online for the do-it-yourself person who follow along to learn the system. Of course, we have the online version like in the example of the woman that I just told you about. We also have a service where they can have weekly calls, and then we take them by the hand, and we counsel them. We have people in Africa and Paris, Belgium; we do Skype. They record themselves exercising; they send it so that I can check their form because the form is very important and guide them and we get amazing results.

I love this business model because it puts you in the driver's seat. It gives you the education that you need to sustain result long term. Because the truth of the matter, how do you want to spend the next 30 years of your life? I mean if you are 50 or 40, 30 years you are going to be 70, 80, 90, how long are we going to be alive? Are you always going to have a personal trainer to hold your hand? We need to have the education so that we can do it at our own time at our place. I love doing this because it is providing the education that the person needs to take care of themselves. It is like teaching the person to fish rather than giving them the fish.

*You are teaching them how to take control of their own body, their health, and their fitness.*

*You customize it for them, and you give them the tools so that they can follow the program and then adapt the program as they go through it. They then can get ongoing support from you if they want to make sure that they are using equipment properly. You are there to help if they get stuck, reach a certain plateau, or there's an injury.*

**Batista Gremaud:** Exactly. There's always a solution. Most people come into the program with muscular imbalances. We all compensate on one side or the other. If you are right-handed, maybe your right side is stronger. Because our program is very balanced, their body goes through an adjustment. For example, if your left side is weaker, now it is going to get stronger, and things are going to balance out. However, through the process of that happening, sometimes there is a pain here, a pain there, because the body is readjusting. So, it is very common for the person to panic and say, oh my god, I got hurt. However, it is not like that; it is the body adapting. It is nice to have the comfort of somebody that's gone through it. As I mentioned, I had so many injuries, trust me I know, I was so scared. However, you keep doing it, you keep doing it, one day you wake up, and the pain is gone. I mean it is amazing.

*You say most people have some imbalances. Can you give me an example how you might go about correcting an imbalance?*

**Batista Gremaud:** Okay, so let's say the person is right-handed and they have obviously a much stronger right arm than left arm. So, let's say we are doing an exercise that requires doing eight repetitions with a certain amount of weight on the right and then eight repetitions of the same exercise on the left. You do eight on the right, eight on the left. The right arm is strong, so we always start with the strong arm. We do not want to say good and bad because we do not want to put that in the mind that there's a bad side. We always start with the stronger side because the muscle has memory and has intelligence. The side that is weaker always wants to catch up on the side that is stronger.

We start with the stronger side to set the pace and set the example. Now, the person does the eight repetitions with that arm, and now they go to the weaker side. They are going to do the same amount of weight, and their goal is going to do the same amount of repetitions. However, now what happens is after four repetitions the weaker arm gives out and can't do anymore.

What do we do? We stop. We do not push. We do not force. We do not try to go through the pain. We do not work to failure. We do not do any of that. We stop. We rest. When that arm is ready to go again, we finish whatever that is. If we had eight and we did four, then we are going to shoot to do four more. Now if after two, that arm says no I cannot do anymore, then you stop at two, you wait again, and when you are ready, you finish so that you have the same amount of repetitions with the same amount of weight on both sides. Eventually, that weaker arm is going to catch up to the other arm, and you are going to achieve balance.

*Okay, that makes sense. Now another question about a point you just made and I want to get some clarity here. You said you do not push to failure. I understand that you do not want to do something that's uncomfortable, but how do you get the adaptive response with the muscle if you do not push it to a certain point where it must adapt?*

**Batista Gremaud:** It is not like we keep it easy and not challenging or any of that. We do not do anything that is uncomfortable, which means that we make sure that all the angles are appropriate so that the body can work biomechanically in the right way. Sometimes we go into a machine, and the machine may not be properly aligned, so there's friction, and then it is hard to do the exercise. Alternatively, there might be a pain in the shoulder where we could change the angle of the exercise. We can bypass the pain because there's always a way to do something where you are not in pain. When we bypass the pain, you start building the synergetic muscles around the injury to fortify it so that now the injury itself is protected, so you do not aggravate it.

That is what I mean by never doing anything that is uncomfortable. However, it does not mean that the person is not encouraged to go past where they think their limit is. In the example that I gave you earlier, the woman that could not get out of bed and she could not lift anything. Her target weight was 25-pound dumb bells, but she could not lift one dumb bell. By making sure she was correctly set up, we told her to do 10 pounds this next week, and then increase to 15.

She said, "I cannot use 15 pounds." So, I replied, "Yes you can because we see that you raised your strength with the leg press from 50 to 100, you can do 15. You could do 20, but we are going to be conservative, do 15." They are encouraged to push the barrier until they reach that weight.

When the person has reached their optimum weight, then the pace changes. Now we lower the weight, we increase the reps, we change their exercise sequence, we go from a dumb bell to a cable, so there's always ways to keep the muscles to readapt and make progress. For me, it is 35-pound dumb bells. When I started, I could not lift five pounds either, I had a frozen shoulder. My target weight is 35 pounds; I am not interested in going any heavier than that.

*We must recognize that everybody has got a different comfort zone or discomfort zone. You are saying that you use progressive resistance based on where you are and what you need to do to get results.*

**Batista Gremaud:**    Exactly. There's a way of manipulating the repetitions and the sets. They do a certain weight with eight reps and then they increase the weight, but decrease the repetitions. Stephen has that down to a science, and that is part of the magic of the programs. How we manipulate the exercises with the weights and the reps results in amazing things.

We worked with a 60-year-old woman. She had never worked out at all in her entire life. We worked with her one-on-one in the gym. On her first day in the gym, she leg-pressed 350 pounds in the first 20 minutes.

*Wow. That is impressive.*

**Batista Gremaud:**    She did it comfortably and laughing. We just worked with somebody who is 74 years old. She is a cancer survivor, she just had heart surgery a few years back, and she is under medical supervision. We also worked with her in the gym one on one, and within the first couple of days in the gym she was also leg-pressing about 350 pounds, comfortably, smiling. When you do it right, and you do it comfortably, it becomes very empowering. What's happening is not only empowering for the body but what we get as a result is it quiets the mind. It is a stress management tool like no other. It is even more powerful than meditation. When you meditate, you sit down, and you let the thoughts come in and out, and you watch your breath. When you lift the weight, it is just you and god. At that moment, you cannot be thinking about other things.

*Batista, you covered quite a bit of ground and have been very great with the examples, but what's one thing that we may not have covered that you could share for women over 40 who are considering starting a fitness program?*

**Batista Gremaud:** Posture is something that people do not think about. Especially when they go into a fitness program. They never give it any thoughts, and I see this in the gyms all the time. People go into machines, exercises or in the yoga classes and they work in the existing posture alignment. They make it worse. Most people do not realize the effect posture has on health is tremendous. Back problem, sciatica, breathing, lungs, and so many things that can be affected by bad posture. So, if you are starting an exercise program, first take a picture of your body sideways, or front, side and back and assess your posture. The first step to improving your fitness is awareness because if you do not know, you cannot do anything about it.

Begin by looking at where your posture is and then whatever you are doing, just try to work against it. Do something to at least try to improve it because you cannot think good posture. I think good posture, but now I am standing straight. Then two minutes later, you are back because you need to build the synergetic muscles in the back, in the shoulders that will hold your posture together. So, you can help yourself by first becoming aware of it and then whatever you are doing, try to work on it so that you start straightening up.

*That is great advice. Batista, if people want to connect with you, learn more about your programs and what you and Stephen are doing, where should they go?*

**Batista Gremaud:**   They can visit our website, and that is drfitnessusa.com. On the home page, you can request a free report. If you are a woman, select the woman report, and then you will receive the free report, and that will put you on our email list where you will receive updates. We are also on social media; we are everywhere.

We have over 300 videos on YouTube at youtube.com/ drfitnessusa

We are very active on Facebook, Facebook/drfitnessusa and on LinkedIn, it is drfitnessusa also, but Stephen is under Stephen Percy, and I am under my name Batista Gremaud. However, if you Google drfitnessusa you can find us everywhere.

The first step though, go to the website and register for a free report.

*The free report contains a lot of good information, and the videos on YouTube are very informative, giving great insight into their approach as well as their personalities and I would recommend that you check them out.*

# About Batista Gremaud

Batista Gremaud is the co-founder of the International Institute of Body Design, most commonly known as Dr Fitness USA. Her passion is helping busy women over forty get 20% stronger in 20 minutes; look and feel 15 years younger and achieve a pain free life with the Body Design Formula Prescription Strength Training System. Certified also in personal training, Batista's expertise in strength training includes structural realignment of the spine and injury prevention.

Batista is a No. 1 Best Selling author and co-creator of the Feminine Body Design prescription strength training coaching system.

Featured guest as an expert authority speaker on the International Pain Foundation,

Batista regularly writes for addiction recovery magazines and online health platforms and has appeared as a celebrity guest speaker on numerous podcasts, radio and tv shows.

A former international performer in ballet, flamenco and Spanish dance Batista Gremaud is a visionary, also certified in hands on healing, intuitive readings and energy clearing. Batista Gremaud 's long time passion in dance, quantum physics and metaphysical science inspires her to help busy women over forty to achieve greater integration of body, mind and spirit through the practice of strengthening the body and the mind with the Feminine Body Design prescription strength training coaching system.

**Business Name**
International Institute of Body Design AKA Dr Fitness USA

**Website**
DrFitnessUSA.com

**Contact**
Batista **at** DrFitnessUSA **dot** com

**Phone**
424-245-6560

**YouTube**
YouTube.com/drfitnessusa

**Facebook Batista**
Facebook.com/FeminineBodyDesign

**Facebook Dr Fitness USA**

Facebook.com/drfitnessusa

**LinkedIn**

LinkedIn.com/in/BatistaGremaud

# Fitness Innovator and Creator of Astro-Durance Total Body Bungee Systems

Patty Cummings is CEO and Creator of Astro-Durance Bungee Systems, the new motion-based bungee exercise training concept and program. Her product is changing lives across the country and the world. People over 40, 50 and older who thought their fitness days were a thing of the past can now experience pain-free and effective fitness training thanks to Patty's creation.

Patty was inspired to develop Astro-Durance Bungee Systems because there was a void in the fitness world for helping people who had physical limitations exercise. Whether it was MS, a stroke, obesity, an amputation, arthritis, or recent surgery, these people had limited or no options for fitness training in a traditional gym setting.

Patty set out to create an exercise experience that would make people feel alive again by giving them the gift of pain-free movement. Patty's creation accomplished this goal and so much more. Men and women of all ages are finding Astro-

Durance fitness programs to be a very challenging, fun and efficient addition to their fitness regimen. Elite athletes are discovering how effective the bungee system is for increasing their endurance, balance, and strength. Children and student-athletes alike can train safely while improving their functional movements and overall fitness.

Although her product just launched in August of 2017, her product is already in 37 states and five countries. As she continues to get more industry and media attention, Patty is gearing up her business to help more people "Feel alive again."

# Conversation with Patty L. Cummings

*To help give a perspective on Astro-Durance, can you describe the journey you took to develop it, and what motivated you to go down that path?*

**Patty Cummings:**　I have always had a passion working with people throughout my life. I started training personally in my hometown of Peoria, Illinois and found many clients had injuries, more injuries than what I realized. When I became a personal trainer, I thought I would be training a lot of athletes and be around healthy people all the time. Well, that was not the case. Many people that were healthy, maybe hurt their ankle or injured their knee or were recovering from breast cancer to hip replacement to back issues, to where you must get more creative now with your workouts. So, your typical type of training changed, and I had to start thinking differently on training them, "Okay, how can I help them do these types of movements without putting the pain on their joints?"

When I moved to Cape Coral, Florida, I started seeing more people in need of help with exercising because they had more issues, and I had to rig things to make it comfortable. Hearing their stories was heartbreaking. They would break down crying and say, "Patty, I can't do this anymore. You don't understand, and I want this so bad, so I am going to hire you to hopefully help me do something." You fall in love with your clients because you get to know who they are, and you start feeling like they are your family and you want to work harder to get them to feel better.

The one thing that I find that is a secret ingredient to making someone successful is confidence. Without confidence, nothing can happen because clients do not feel it within themselves. I had to figure out how do I make people feel confident in themselves? When I saw Cirque du Soleil, it dawned on me. For over 30 years, they have been using a bungee product in the air for acrobatic movements. Why are they not doing this for fitness? When I started researching what they do for beautiful dancing, this swan style, then I had nothing to go off. I searched and searched, and there was nothing out there. So, I just started creating and tried to figure out, how can I do this? What can I do?

Finally, I started putting parts together and rigging things. You would've laughed if you would've seen what the first pieces looked like, but it was working, and that is all I cared about. I tried thinking like Edison with the light bulb theory. He went through how many failures before he finally got it? It was the same thing. People were telling me, "Well, they are doing that in the dance," and it is not the same. These people are not 90 pounds and fit and soaring in the air. People need help, so it is a whole different type of setup that you must put together. How do we determine how much weight of resistance to use? Everyone is a different weight. Everyone is a different size. So, if someone weighs 200 pounds, we need something that's 250 pounds that can hold them up.

Throughout all the testing, I remade this product four different times. Finally, I realized, "Here we go, we got this. We've got buoyancy. We can add weight; we can remove weight. Let's make this simple and easy." Now I have my product and I have clients that felt like they could never do something again gaining confidence within themselves and are now doing things. The biggest thing for some people is to be able to do a push-up. Many women cannot do push-ups.

There are also women that could once do push-ups, but cannot do them anymore because of a shoulder issue or something happened to them, so that strength is gone.

What a confidence builder it is putting them on this product and having them do a push-up. They feel good. Now they feel strong. Now they feel inspired. Now they are like, "What else can I do?" Then the game is on. They say, "Let's start training." Why? Because they feel good. They are laughing. They are smiling. Their confidence is coming back. They are loving fitness again because there's no pain in their joints whatsoever.

That is how it began, and here we are today, a year and a half later. We have blown up worldwide, and now we are getting in rehabilitation centers. I am working with several doctors, chiropractors, and we work with athletes to go the next level of training for high endurance.

*You talked about the challenge of giving clients confidence, and the fact that people need confidence before they can do some of the more advanced exercises. Where did you start in building that confidence?*

**Patty Cummings:**  I would talk with my client, and find out what kind of medications they are on, what kind of surgeries they have had, and where are their aches and pains. Then I would say, "I would like you to give me the opportunity to show you something. However, you must trust the product because it is very difficult in the beginning because you are suspended in the air. You may even think, 'Is this thing really going to hold me up?'" As a trainer, I always stand right next to my client to assure them, "I am not leaving you, I am right next to your side." We weigh them of course to make sure we use the proper amount of resistance to support them. If they weigh 160 pounds, I use 200 pounds of resistant bungee on them. We have an additional 40 pounds of product to suspend them up in the air.

When I get them on the product, I have them start with squats first. I tell them to just act like you are sitting in the chair, push your hips back and squat down to the ground and come up. It is funny because I love to see their face at first. They look at me like, "Honey, I can't do squats," or "It has been a long time since I have done squats." Others say, "Ooh, squats will hurt my knees." I tell them, "That is right, but you are going to finally do a squat with *no pain.* You can do a squat with this product. So, let's just try it." They will look at me, and then they go down, and they do a squat. Their eyes get big, they rise, and they smile, and that is what I look for.

When I see that smile, I know that they are feeling good now within themselves. Then I say, "Okay, now let's go for nine more. You can do this," and my clients do nine more. Sometimes clients grab their hands, wrap their fingers around each other, and they go to their chest, and say, "I can't believe I just did a squat. I did squats. I had no pain. What the heck? What just happened?" I am like, "Ta-da! That is what just happened. Magic. Isn't this beautiful?" Then they respond, "Can I try it again?" They usually want to do it again because they cannot believe what they just did. I then go into the next phase which is lunges which are very difficult to do.

*I agree. How do you help your clients perform lunges?*

**Patty Cummings:** We even help people with severe knee injuries perform lunges. When someone with a knee injury performs a lunge; they cannot believe they just did the perfect lunge. Then I have them do ten more lunges. When they do ten, I know that I have them, because they are so happy and they believe in the product. They believe in the product because squats and lunges are two of the most difficult exercises for people with knee pain or other medical issues. Once they see that they can do those two, they now trust you, and they trust the product. They are feeling confident now, and that is what's so important. Then I love to show them how they can feel airborne with soft jumps. Many people cannot jump today because of the impact, so I have them always put themselves in a 45-degree angle, feeling the resistance of the bungee on the balls of their feet.

For the first time in fitness, clients can stand on the balls of their feet and stretch almost all the 687 muscles in their body. All those muscles are being stretched out, seriously being stretched out. Everything is lining up perfectly. The form's perfect. Now, I ask them to jump softly on the balls of their feet. They start laughing, and say, "Oh my gosh, this does not hurt. It is magic, it is magical." I hear this all the time, freedom. They feel free. Training for the first time and they have no pain, but it works.

People wonder, "What am I going to get out of that?" You are going to get more out of this training than any other training out there, because now for the first time, you are training your body organically. We are always talking about eating organically and living organically. However, the way we train our bodies is not very organic because of all the impact on the joints. We are hard on our bodies. Our bodies are not meant to handle that much impact. So, in due time, we will suffer. We may look beautiful today, but later down the road, we are going to have a lot of aches and pains, and we are going to suffer.

However, now with this product, you can train organically and get that type of toning and weight loss and go back in bio time, feeling young again.

*What does organic training mean to the average person?*

**Patty Cummings:** Organic training to me is having a healthy body. That is my definition based on this product with the discoveries I have made using it. To me, the secret to a healthy body is the lymphatic system. Many people do not know what the lymphatic system is. They have heard of it, but they do not know the definition, so I highly recommend people to research the lymphatic system. The lymphatic system is what helps cleans all the toxins and the waste out of the body.

As we get older, the lymphatic system starts to slow down. I use the analogy of a stopping point. When we are young, we feel good, and we have the freedom of running and jumping. Adults look at kids and say, "Gosh, I wish I had their energy." When you are young, you have that lymphatic system going throughout the body. Then behind the lymphatic system is the blood flow. With the blood, you have oxygen, so everything is just moving right. The blood and oxygen are just flowing, your metabolism is on a high, burning your calories, you feel good. However, as we get older, our biological systems start slowing down. When we sustain injuries, they start slowing down even more, and it results in the oxygen not pumping like it was. The lymphatic system is at a stopping point.

With Astro-Durance, you can get that lymphatic system revving back up through the body again. When that happens, the blood starts flowing with oxygen pumping through the body. What we are finding is it like going back in "bio-time." With the lymphatic system operating properly, it is starting to clean out the body by getting rid of those toxins and the waste. These are my theories based on what we are finding. For example, people sometimes get a headache when they first start. Their headache will last 15 to 20 minutes. Why are they getting the headache? It is because they are getting oxygen put back in their brain, and that is a good thing because we start lacking oxygen. Now we are getting oxygen pumping back in, and it is starting to heal our clients from a lot of their aches and pains.

We have so many clients using the product who have medical issues, from arthritis to MS to Parkinson's. Once they get on the product, they give us testimonials and videos for us because they are becoming pain-free. Now, can I guarantee everybody with symptoms that this is a cure-all? No, I cannot, but what I can tell you is that in our discoveries that you can finally train again, start healing your body again, and love what you are doing in fitness. It is not tearing you up. It is not hurting you. Therefore, I feel like this is organic training.

On top of this, you are getting endorphins and you are happy. You are also stretching every muscle in the body for the first time in fitness. Go back to when you were training. For the first time in fitness, when you are training on this apparatus, you found every muscle stretching as you are toning and pumping those muscles.

And, you had no pain. When you finished, did you feel taller? Did you feel light? How did you feel when you got off the apparatus of the Astro-Durance Bungee Systems?

*I felt great. I had a great workout; I was drenched in sweat after only 30 minutes. I did feel like I'd stretched everything out and felt taller. Afterward, I felt very good, very enjoyable; it is what I call a workout high. I think one of the things my wife said, which was very revealing to me was, she says, "I don't like doing squats. I don't like doing push-ups, but I liked them today," and she laughed. She was honest; she does not like them. I think what amazed me about the workout is the fact that it was fun! It was a challenging workout where. I was using a variety of muscles running, jumping and squatting and I never found myself thinking, "Oh my gosh, I have to do three more reps!" To be honest, it felt like being a kid again.*

*What I am finding with older adults is that they are suffering chronic diseases because of their sedentary life. They are sedentary either by choice, an injury or because of medications or other illnesses. Because they are sedentary, they are not using their muscles which results in atrophy. If they do go to the gym to work out, they often rely on machines. Although this provides some fitness benefits and can build muscle, it does not work the entire body or activate the lymphatic system. The fact that your product works the whole body and facilitates pain-free movement is a very, very, very powerful way of getting people enjoyably engaged and back into fitness. Because if they do it and they enjoy it, they will continue to do it.*

*What I want to explore now is the type of people who are using this product. You have many people using the product who normally don't go to gyms. They are the people who have given up and said, "Hey, there is no way I am going to work out, it hurts too much." How do you get those people to find you so that they can experience the Astro-Durance system?*

**Patty Cummings:** Many people found me by watching videos and reading clientele testimonies on Facebook. The great thing about the product is that it helps all types of clients. I am hitting many categories with this product. You can do gymnastics. You can do dance. You can do athletes. You can do injured. It works with people who are overweight. I would ask every client to do a testimonial. How did that feel, what did you think? My clients' successes helped bring me my new clients.

I love the baby boomers. I love everybody, don't get me wrong, but the baby boomers are loyal. They show up. They want to take care of themselves. They do not want the aches and pains, and they are willing to try to figure out if there is something new that can help them get rid of the pain.

Once you get a baby boomer seeing that they can feel alive again and having that taste of freedom, they bring their friends with them. Their friends are saying, "What are you doing? You are not the same. Look at how well you are moving and getting up." My clients tell their friends, "It sounds crazy, but I am on a bungee." So, their friend comes with them the next time.

I have been in restaurants and have overheard people talking about my product, and I smile when I eat because it feels really good. I love hearing what they say. So, it also word of mouth. Facebook helps, but the biggest thing is if the people believe in your product, which they will because it works, their friends start seeing the results, and they are going to follow. I know if I see my girlfriend and we are the same age, and her face is looking flawless, I ask, "Where are you going?" "Oh, I am going to the skin center down here. They have a new product they put on the face," I am going to go try that cream because I see her results and they look amazing.

We also have your in-betweeners, which is more my age. They want that harder feel, high endurance training, so they regularly run five or ten miles. They love what is called runner's high. I want to give them that runner's high, and I am going to have them run on this product. Imagine you weigh 160 pounds, and we have got 200 pounds of resistance behind you, and you are running against 200 pounds trying to pull you back. They do five of those runs with high jumps and they are out of breath. I love it when they are done after just five runs, which is 30 seconds. They are now puddling in sweat. So, I must teach them how to re-breathe. They are trying to figure out, "How did this happen? When I run five miles, I don't get this exhausted."

*The 30 seconds of sprints were very, very intense. They took me to the max cardiovascularly, and I needed a recovery period of 15, 20 seconds before I could do it again. The product is not just for people with limitations. For instance, my wife was doing a basic push-up, and then Brooke said, "You can try some hand clap push-ups, and then let's try some explosive push-ups." Brooke was able to adapt it to different levels with us both working out. Both of us getting a good workout for our level and interest. I am saying, "More, more, more," and my wife is saying, "Hey, this is pretty good. I am doing something I have never done before," and that is cool.*

**Patty Cummings:** Correct. She was modified and you went to a different level. She felt so good just to do a push-up, and you felt good doing an explosion, so both of your confidence meters were rising high. What happened to you is a perfect example of how word of mouth works with this product. When you went back home, you shared it with your daughter, and I am sure now your daughter has a taste on her tongue like, "Gosh, Dad, I want to try this." It is the same thing when we get athletes in here; they lead other runners to come in by telling them about their experience. So now they are on it. We have taken athletes to the next level within a matter of months. We both know the secret to go to the next level in anything we do in fitness; from young to elderly, you must have endurance.

Endurance is very hard to get. We are taught that you must feel it, hurt, hurt, hurt, hurt, hurt. If you are not hurting, it is not working, and that is not the case today. Today, you can keep going and going. For the first time in fitness, your body is like a spring, like a kangaroo. It does not want to stop, but internally your cardio is saying, "Whoa." We are talking within a matter of seconds; it is telling me to stop. However, you want to keep doing those squats or those burpees.

For the first time, you are doing burpees and you have no pain, and you are doing them perfectly. It's like you are airborne and floating in a cloud, and you are coming down and coming up, and you are smiling, and you feel good, but suddenly, you feel like, "I cannot breathe! What the heck?" So now, for the first time in fitness, it is the complete opposite. That is why people are scratching their head because 30, 40, 50, 60, 70 years or however many years of experience you have in fitness, you are thinking, "This is not what I am used to. It is not what I know. It is not what I was taught." I mean, am I correct? Is that how you felt?

*That is correct. One of the things I wanted to build on is the fact that you recommend only a 30-minute workout. Why is that?*

**Patty Cummings:** That is all you need because the endurance is so intense. We are going on a ten count because the endurance is that intense. I use analogies for people to understand. Pretend you have a big man. We will use someone like Lou the Hulk and he is holding behind your shirt, and you are trying to run from him. Imagine running, you have got this big musclebound guy behind you holding you from behind by that shirt, and you are trying to run and get away. It is the same thing with the resistant bands. We are adding more intensity, more resistant bands on it. You are trying to escape away from it, but it is pulling you back.

So, for the first time in fitness, you are using all your core to hold against that resistance and to start moving those muscles. What's so beautiful is the way I have designed it and created it, your form is usually always perfect. You are always properly aligned. So, whatever you are working, you are not hunched over, you are not in a curve, you are perfectly aligned as you are training that body.

You are now getting that high endurance training because it is pulling you away as you are using that core to stay forward in the 45-degree angle. Even when you are doing jumping jacks, you feel like you are on a cloud because you are at a 45-degree angle. However, once again, you have got that 200 pounds pulling you back. Using that core strength to stay forward, you are going to be out of breath because it is all cardio. Ten seconds is all you need, and then you break for 10. Then you do another 10.

Some people can pass out on you, and you must watch them and watch their coloring. Do not overdo it. I have had athletes do two more runs, and suddenly, they are about to pass out. We would put liquid sugar or honey underneath their tongue, which brings you back within seconds. They look at you like, "I did not expect that." There's a reason why we tell you we start with five runs. We want to hear every client count while they are training, so we can hear how they are breathing. When they get to, "Five, six," I usually tell them to stop. We do not go to ten, and we take a break for a second.

*In addition to doing the cardiovascular types of workout, you can also do weight training. Can you tell us about that?*

**Patty Cummings:**  Men and women love lifting weights with the product. Once again, it is training organically, because, for the first time, we put them in a 45-degree angle doing exercises like dumbbells curls, hammers curls, frontal raises, and lateral raises. However, the weight is going to feel heavier. 20 pounds now feel like 40 pounds. You will only need half the normal weight to get results. Our guys and girls are toned. They train organically now suspended on the product with weights. They do press squats, and their other exercises, all on the product because they are stretching their muscles as they are building their muscles. It is mind-blowing what people are doing with this, and I love seeing it.

The guys love it. They are heavy lifting on this product. Then they get off the product, and they do it freestanding with no product on them, and say, "Patty, I can see where my form is off, and I am hunching over. No wonder my back kills me. On the product, it kept my back nice and aligned when I am lifting." Or, the hips are back where they should be. Their feet are nice and aligned on the floor, and how they should be, and when they get off, and they train, they see such a huge difference.

*Proper body alignment is so critical when it comes to lifting weights. If you do not use proper form, that is when an injury happens. If you are getting back into fitness, the last thing you want to do is to get injured and then not be able to work out. The idea of safety is one of the key issues for people, especially over 50, that want to work out. They want a challenge, but they do not want to get hurt. Astro-Durance is a vehicle where they can challenge themselves, they can be safe, and they can return to the gym the next day if they desire.*

**Patty Cummings:** Exactly, and I am telling you, once you start training this way, you do not want to go back the other way, because you feel good, and that is what it should be about.

I am getting older. I am 46, and I tore my knee out when I was doing basic plyometric exercises not too long ago with a client. I had to get on my apparatus, and I started working it, trying to get it back to normal. I am so used to training a certain way on Astro, but I need to remember that I can't when I get off Astro. I was mad because I was down for quite a few months. I called it knee Tourette's because I would be talking and then if I moved it the wrong way, it was such severe pain, I would be like, "Ah, oh my gosh!" I finally understand what people go through when they talk about a severe knee injury. It is horrible.

I got on my Astro product and worked it out without needing to have surgery. I cannot wait for the day when other people will have the choice of how they would like to train. We are growing so fast and I am hoping people in every city have an opportunity to try this product and make discoveries for themselves. Then they can see which way they like, they now have a choice, which is nice.

*How did you come up with the name Astro-Durance?*

**Patty Cummings:** When I created the product, I wanted a name that was original and unique to the experience it gave people. To me, it felt like I was floating. It reminded me of when I was growing up and would see the astronauts floating in their spaceship. Then I thought about endurance, so I combined them and came up with Astro-Durance.

"Astro Hero" is one of the terms we use for our trainers, and it is what is listed on the back of their shirts.

*Patty, you have been involved in the medical field with your P2 Personal Training facility and using the Astro-Durance Bungee System to help patients recover from surgery and other physical limitations. You also recently joined forces with David and Kendra Lyons, and their MS Fitness Challenge, a 501(c)(3) charity that provides fitness programs, encouragement, and services for people with Multiple Sclerosis. What does that mean to you and your organization?*

**Patty Cummings:**    Partnering with David is huge for me. I was so happy. It was such a blessing and a dream come true. David is an amazing man. He and his wife are a great team, and I was praying that he was going to get involved with me, and he is busy with so many people coming at him. We talked, and after he looked at everything and worked with everything, he was just blown away.

Since then, we are constantly working on projects, and putting things together. We want to go out there together and start saving lives. We want to start healing people and showing them; you can train again. We can work through this. Watch what this will do. I am flying out to LA in two weeks to meet his whole team. I am even going to meet Lou Ferrigno, the Hulk, which is going to be exciting. David Lyons is doing a new TV fitness series, and we are looking to put our apparatus in one of his episodes for the fall. We are also looking at an MS challenge with this. I am very excited to see what he has put together when I get there.

What I love about David is he has passion. He has a lot coming at him. He has been a very successful man his whole life, and then he wound up getting MS himself. He saw for the first time, like me with the knee injury, what it was like to have pain that you have never endured before in your life. When he told me his story, it was very touching. He was in the hospital, and they thought he had a brain tumor. They were going to give him brain surgery, and he had two options. He would be in a wheelchair, or he could die. Well, then he passed on the surgery and said, "I am not getting brain surgery." A few months later, a new doctor diagnosed him with MS.

They told David that with MS, "You will never walk again. You will be in a wheelchair the rest of your life." David, and I love his mind, the power of the mind is everything, said, "Not me." The doctors said, "Yes, this is what's going to happen." They put him in a wheelchair and took him to the exit sign. While he was waiting to be picked up, he got up out of the wheelchair and said, "I will not be in a wheelchair," and he walked to the car in pain, he said, dying pain. He was going to prove them wrong. From that point on, he endured much pain, and he made many sacrifices, but he was working out and working out through the pain to show people, you can fight this.

Even with the MS pain, he was enduring; he was training other clients suffering from the same pain. He put his pain aside to help the person in front of him. To me, that is so heroic and so passionate. How can you not want to partner up with someone like that? We are not out here to make money. We are here to change people's lives, and with him being on my team, with whom he brings to the table and what I bring to the table, this is a win-win. We are going to go out there, and we are going to change the world, and I am excited because I want to see people have confidence again. I want to see people live with a smile and knowing they can walk again.

We have had so many people that have had strokes, and their physical therapists have brought them to us, and within a matter of weeks, we have gotten their body parts moving again. Not a year, not two years. Within weeks, because they can be lifted and suspended and start working that area, and they have no pain in that area. So now we start getting the lymphatic system moving, that blood flowing, the oxygen pumping, pumping that muscle, start working it, and then before you know it, they have got movement.

Donna, our latest stroke client, has been with us seven weeks now, and her speech is completely clear. You need watch the first video when she came here and compare it to where she is now to appreciate how far she has come. She is moving her leg completely. Moving it forward, and to the side. She is walking backwards. She is now walking without her brace. She trains without her brace. She comes in without a walker. She has a cane, but many times she walks without the cane, but she keeps it there for her balance and support. Her arm is getting movement again. It is mind-blowing on what this is doing.

David and I are doing a medical conference in September, to show physical therapists, chiropractors, and trainers what this product does and how it can benefit their clients instantly. People do not have two years to heal. They have today. We want what's going to work for us now. This product will start working immediately, and that is what people need. I am very thankful and very proud to say David Lyons is on our team to help make things happen.

*With his passion and yours, I can imagine the numbers of people that you are going to be able to and help. Because of the tremendous prescriptive value of movement, the more you move the better you feel. The better you feel, the more you move. Movement is the greatest prescription for what ails us, and your product gives people the gift of pain-free movement.*

*Movement is a gift that we should never take for granted. Some people lose their movement permanently because they give up. They gave up because of the pain, frustration, and inconvenience. Your product gives those people hope and options, and if they want to take that option, then they can get movement, and they can accomplish their fitness goals in a way that they never would've been able to before.*

*Patty, if people want to explore that option, learn more about the Astro-Durance Bungee System and contact you, where should they go?*

**Patty Cummings:** They can go to astrodurance.com, A-S-T-R-O-D-U-R-A-N-C-E dot com, and on our website, we have a lot to offer there. Our contact information is on there, and they can check us out on Facebook.

## About Patty L. Cummings

Patty Cummings, entrepreneur, owns Astro-Durance Bungee Studios (Formerly P2 Personal Training); she is a Fitness Educator; Public Speaker; Inventor; CEO and Creator of Astro-Durance Bungee Systems, the new motion-based bungee exercise training concept, and program. She has been featured in USA Today; Fox 4; CBS; and is presently working with a new television series "Pumped - the Muscle Hustle" to be aired January 2019. Patty supports the charity efforts of David and Kendra Lyons, Founders of MS Fitness Challenge, a 501C3 non- profit that helps those with Multiple Sclerosis and other physical limitations.

Ms. Cummings is an extraordinary entrepreneur who successfully invented, created, and launched a ground-breaking bungee fitness system in August of 2017 and teaches one-day and two-day workshops for Astro-Durance Bungee training certification and business classes on how to start a bungee business.

After launching Astro-Durance Bungee Systems in August 2017, she immediately gained attention from medical professionals and Iconic leaders in the bodybuilding and fitness industry for her result-oriented product. Astro-Durance Motion-Based Bungee Training is revolutionizing the way the world views exercise and is presently in 37 states, and five countries - Turkey, Australia, Costa Rica, Canada and South Africa - with more nations pending.

Patty Is the mother of four, a daughter 26, Son 22, and twin boys age 11. Her motto is "Feel Alive" and "I can, and I will!" Her positive attitude and motivating personality is an inspiration to others and one of her greatest assets.

She has a lot of great projects in the works for the future.

**Website**
astrodurance.com
p2personaltraining.com

**Email**
pattyc@astrodurance.com

**Location**
334 Nicholas Pkwy NW, Suite D
Cape Coral, FL 33991

**Facebook**
Facebook.com/AstroDurance/?ref=br_rs
Facebook.com/p2training/

# 'Easy Prey' Author Shares Insight into Cybersecurity and IT Services for Ultimate Peace of Mind

Darren Coleman has spent his career taking the mystery out of information technology. He is a passionate information technology professional, entrepreneur, and technology author based in Langley, British Columbia, Canada. Currently, he is the president and certified IT administration for Coleman Technologies, which he founded in 1999. Throughout the span of nearly two decades, Darren has acquired extensive expertise in the world of information technology and has directly worked with some of the top real estate franchises in the nation.

As a technical specialist in a multitude of areas, his key forte lies in consulting, IT management services, computer security, and more. Darren's avid interest in technology has led to his extensive training and many certifications in areas such as information technology and computer support specialist, Certified Ethical Hacker, and Datto Certified Advanced

Technician. He also possesses the CompTIA A+ and CompTIA Network+ qualification and Darren has completed extensive training in Linux administration and configuration.

When he isn't immersed in his career, Darren enjoys traveling and spending time outdoors with his family and friends. Most importantly, Darren enjoys nothing more than spending quality time with his lovely wife and children. He and his wife are the proud parents of three beautiful girls. Darren was a featured speaker at the Harvard Business Expert Forum at Harvard Faculty Club. He is an author in two No. 1 bestselling books, "Easy Prey: How to Protect Your Business from Data Breach, Cybercrime, and Employee Fraud," and "Thought Leaders: Business Expert Forum at Harvard Faculty Club."

## Conversation with Darren Coleman

*Who Do You Help?*

**Darren Coleman:** We help any small business owner or manager who's tired of dealing with computer problems, any small business owner or manager who has a network that runs slow or acts crazy, or really any business owner who's worried about data loss, viruses, and keeping their network safe from hackers. Over the years, we have helped major real estate, law, and financial firms.

*What do you think is the biggest issue facing business people today related to their computers?*

**Darren Coleman:** The biggest issue today would be cybercrime, ransomware, and hackers. You can't set up your computer and connect it to the Internet and never touch it again.

That is a surefire path to disaster.

For example, compare your computer network to your car. Your car will drive for a long time without maintenance of any kind. You can even ignore changing the tires, or the oil, or any type of regular maintenance before you end up broken down. Unfortunately, if you wait till your car literally stops running, you are going to incur far more charges, towing and repairs, and getting it back on the road, not to mention the hassle of being without your car for that time.

Your network is just like that. Most business owners don't have anyone monitoring or doing maintenance for their network. It works fine until some major crash or problem occurs. Then they end up with downtime, and it costs them a few thousand dollars to get it back up. Even then, they might end up losing data that can't be recovered. They might end up ruining client relationships because a hacker has accessed their client's credit card data, or simply spammed them with a nasty virus from their server. Of course, maintenance is going to make their network run a lot more faster and it's going to be more stable, and they won't get the surprise of failure or other problems nearly as often. Again, the biggest mistake many business owners make is thinking that everything is running OK, and they don't need to invest a little bit of time or money to keep their network maintained and their data secure.

*What are some of the consequences of lack of maintenance, security, and network downtime?*

**Darren Coleman:** As a small business owner, you are always under attack. There are well-funded cyber rings in China, Russia, and the Ukraine, and they're using sophisticated software to hack thousands of businesses. They steal credit cards and customer information. Don't think because you are small that you are immune to it. Big companies such as The Home Depot and J.P. Morgan are in the news, but the small businesses are the ones paying the price every day.

*When people work with you, why do you think that most people choose you and your company over other people or companies? Why would they become your customer?*

**Darren Coleman:** We knew that we had to find a better way to deliver regular critical monitoring and maintenance to our clients that allowed us to monitor their networks 24/7 because everyone is vulnerable to cybercrime, hacking, and viruses all the time. We also knew we had to make it very affordable. What we've done is we invested in a new technology that allows us to automate a large portion of the maintenance and the monitoring.

We proactively manage our customers' computer networks to eliminate many of the headaches and hassles of using computers to run a business. In addition, we guarantee our customers a response within 90 minutes or less, and we're the only IT service provider in the region that offers a 100 percent no-hassle, money-back guarantee on our flat rate all-inclusive service plans.

We call it the Full Fixed Fee program. The single biggest benefit to our clients would be peace of mind. They pay one flat monthly fee, and we provide them with a combination of on-site and remote support for their network to make sure it's not only just performing at peak performance, but also that data is secured and protected from hackers, viruses, spyware, spam, and hardware failure, and even employee sabotage. We make sure that backups are functioning, that virus definitions are up-to-date and constantly updated. Plus, we make sure the firewall is configured properly, and that the server is functioning properly.

*Since peace of mind is important for people today, how do you provide backup, security and full protection for clients as a safety net?*

**Darren Coleman:** To illustrate, we have a pie chart that is a bundle of different pieces that are required for technology to operate efficiently. You get the full pie. We call it "all bases covered." We take the initiative with your network. We do your vendor management, your professional services, and your security management. We even do business cloud hosting, backup and disaster recovery. We make sure all the bases are covered for our clients.

*What are some of the popular misconceptions about the services that you provide?*

**Darren Coleman:** Here is an embarrassing and little known fact about the IT industry. It's not regulated.

Many other professional service industries are regulated, which means anyone can claim that they're a computer repair expert. In fact, a lot of these business owners started because they got fired or laid off from their job and they couldn't find work anywhere else. That means that many of these so-called experts are useless, and they make sleazy auto repair shops look like the pinnacles of virtue and competence. Auto repair shops, electricians, plumbers, lawyers, doctors, dentists, accountants, they're all heavily regulated to protect the consumer from receiving poor work or getting ripped off.

In contrast, the computer industry is highly ***unregulated***, and there aren't any laws in existence to protect the consumer. Basically, anyone can hang a shingle outside and promote themselves as an expert.

*Since cybersecurity is an unregulated industry, how important is having certifications? Does having certifications make a difference for your clients?*

**Darren Coleman:** Even if they're honestly trying to help you, and do a good job for you, an uncertified technician's inexperience can cost you dearly in your network speed and performance, or lost or corrupt data. We're different because we've been around for about 20 years. I have contributed to the No. 1 bestselling book, "Easy Prey: How to Protect Your Business from Data Breach, Cybercrime, and Employee Fraud," as well as being featured in the No. 1 bestselling book, "Thought Leaders: Business Expert Forum at Harvard Faculty Club."

I personally train all my technicians, and I make sure they are fully certified. This makes a huge difference.

*Why do you think that some people don't think they need what you have to offer?*

**Darren Coleman:** Sometimes the client just doesn't see the value in the program, and they just don't want to make the commitment. For these clients, we allow them to sign up, and try us out for three months.

At the end of those three months, if they're not absolutely convinced the service is worth every penny, they can contact us and we'll issue a complete refund. That way, there's nothing for them to risk. We're very confident that our clients are going to immediately see the value. If not, we'll part friends. We help our clients with technologies, but we're also helping them with business because the technology drives the business. I don't want our clients to think of us as just the guys who come in and fix the computer. We're actually part of their business success as well.

*What would the process be to get started working with you?*

**Darren Coleman:** Reach out to us by phone at 604-513-9428, or through our website at colemantechnologies.com. Once we have that initial conversation, we're going to make sure that we're a good fit. We're going to start gathering all the information that we require to ensure that you have as little to no downtime as possible.

*You guarantee your work and your also respond to your customers within 90 minutes, can you discuss that?*

**Darren Coleman:** Yes. We have a system for clients to get in touch with us should they have any issue 24/7. They can pick up the phone and call us, or send an email to support. We even have an agent icon that runs on every workstation that we maintain. They can just click on the icon in their task bar and say, "Hey, guys, the computer is not working right. Please connect," and within minutes we take over the session on the computer, and we fix the problem.

*Are most of the computers that you work on, are they all PCs, or do you work with some Mac computers, too? What typically is that scenario?*

**Darren Coleman:** The majority of the business computers we maintain would be Windows-based PCs, either Windows 7, or Windows 10, and so on. But more and more people have Apple products. We will provide limited support for the Apple computers. We actually can monitor and maintain them in the same way we can the Windows computers.

*Can you connect with your clients virtually, so if they're having some type of a computer problem, you can actually go in and fix it right there without actually sending a technician to their location?*

**Darren Coleman:** Most of the service work is done remotely. Not only that, if you think about it, a lot of times during the day the employees are working, and we don't want to kick the employees off the computer because now the business owner is suffering a loss in productivity. With our program, we can even go behind the scenes and work on the computer at the same time that the employee is using the computer without kicking them off. Of course, if we can't do that, we can also connect after hours and on weekends when the computer is not in use.

A lot of the things we do are proactive. We monitor the computer systems, so we know if something might fail in the future, so we can take proactive measures.

*If you were to give some tips about what a business owner can do today to protect themselves from cybercrime or hacking, what would you say?*

**Darren Coleman:** Number one: Know cybercrime, hacking, or virus attacks will happen to you. This means be aware that you will probably get a computer virus, be hacked, or just break down during the normal course of business. Whether it's happened to you in the past or not at all, you're a sitting duck, or easy prey. It's going to happen at some point because it's just so prevalent.

I have a few tips that can help you have more peace of mind.

First, a business owner can protect themselves by having up-to-date systems, and the latest version of Windows or the latest version of Mac. Install the updates when they come out because usually the attacks are because they're attacking a flaw within the system itself. If you keep those up-to-date, that's going to be most important and help protect you.

Second, make sure you have good antivirus software on all your computers. And third, have a perimeter firewall to be analyzing all the traffic coming in and out of your network.

Those three things are going to help you, but the biggest threat to your business is your employees lack of understanding of how viruses and hackers work.

The number one tip related to employees that I could offer would be employee training and education. We do one-to-one training. When we work with a business, we talk to everyone during the on-boarding process to make sure every employee from the top down knows exactly what to do for safe operations. For example, we do some basic training to make sure that each employee knows what to look for when an email comes in, that they don't open the attachment or they don't click the link. We always tell our customers, "If you're ever not sure, that's what you're paying us for. Pick up the phone, give us a call." We'll make sure we steer them in the correct direction.

*If somebody wants to talk to you or get in contact with you, how can they do that?*

**Darren Coleman:** If they're local, they can call us at 604-513-9428. We also do work remotely. You can contact us toll free at 1-800-709-3665. Visit the website, we have tons of free resources, e-books, all sorts of different things that they might want to check out at ColemanTechnologies.com.

There's a contact form that they can contact the company. Check us out on Facebook, LinkedIn, and Twitter. We're everywhere. If you search for Coleman Technologies, we're very big into social media. You should find us at the top of the search results.

Even if someone is not ready to commit as a customer, but just has questions, give me a call. I'll give them some advice, free of charge, of course.

*Where can people find your best-selling book and listen to your interview?*

**Darren Coleman:** You can find "Easy Prey" on Amazon at https://www.amazon.com/Easy-Prey-Worlds-Leading-Experts-ebook/dp/B01I0QTHYK and you can listen to this interview at https://businessinnovatorsradio.com/darren-coleman-easy-prey-author-shares-insight-cyber-security/

# About Darren Coleman

Darren Coleman is the owner of Coleman Technologies located in Langley, BC, Canada. Coleman is a passionate information technology professional, entrepreneur and technology author based in British Columbia. He founded Coleman Technologies in 1999, and since that time has prided himself on his high-quality services across a range of areas. These include consulting, IT management services, computer security, and more. In addition to this, he has achieved certifications as an Information Technology and Computer Support Specialist, as a Certified Ethical hacker, and a Datto Certified Advanced Technician. He has been featured on ABC, NBC, CBS, FOX and CW.

**Location**
Langley, British Columbia, Canada

**Website**
ColemanTechnologies.com

**Email**
darren@coleman.biz

**Phone**
(604)-513-9428

**Facebook**
Facebook.com/ColemanBiz

**LinkedIn**
LinkedIn.com/in/DarrenQColeman

**YouTube**
YouTube.com/user/ColemanTechnologies

.

www.ingramcontent.com/pod-product-compliance
Lightning Source LLC
Chambersburg PA
CBHW071208200326

41519CB00018B/5427